India - China Relations

Problems and Prospects

India - China Relations

Problems and Prospects

Edited By

Prof. Bina Rai

Principal,
Avadh Girls' Degree College,
Lucknow

Dr. Babita Maji

Assistant Professor
Department of Political Science
R.G.(P.G.) College, Meerut

Raj Publications

New Delhi - 110002

India - China Relations: Problems and Prospects

First Published in 2022

ISBN 978-93-92066-04-7

₹ 795

Published by : **Raj Publications**

108, 4855/24, Ansari Road,

Daryaganj, New Delhi-110002

Tel. : 9811010939

E-Mail: rajpublications@yahoo.co.in

Laser Typesetting : Aarati Computers, Delhi-110 009

Printed at : Balaji Offset, Delhi

Contents

Preface

As key emerging powers in the international system, India and especially China have received much attention in recent times. The likely emergence of China and India as new major global players – similar to the rise of Germany in the 19th century and the United States in the early 20th century – will transform the geopolitical landscape, with impacts potentially as dramatic as those of the previous two centuries. In the same way that commentators refer to the 1900s as the "American Century," the early 21st century may be seen as the time when some in the developing world, led by China and India, come into their own. A combination of sustained high economic growth, expanding military capabilities, active promotion of high technologies and large populations will be at the root of the expected rapid rise in economic and political power for both countries.

Relations between the two Asian giant, India and China. have experienced profound upheaval over the past five decades, ranging from benign warmth in the 1950s and hyper-tension in the 1960s and 1970s, to rapprochement in the 1980s and readjustment in the 1990s. A close examination of Chinese and Indian perspectives on the fundamentals of the emerging international order reveals that Sino-Indian differences on many issues of both bilateral and global significance are stark. The major problems in India-China relations are the unresolved border issue that is getting more complicated with increasing Chinese military capability in Pakistan occupied Kashmir (POK); Sino-Pak military nuclear and missile collaboration; and China's String of Pearls strategy to encircle India.

Nevertheless, from the Indian and Chinese point of view, the relationship between them has a global significance. The real significance of India-China relations lies in the significant role that both countries can play in the twenty-first century. However, the global significance of this bilateral relation has been overshadowed by the prolonged issue of border dispute. The border issue is at the core of India's mistrust of China and the uncertainty about its future intentions. Both sides after several rounds of bilateral dialogue have an unsettled 3000 kilometers plus long border. This is creating a recipe for instability, tensions and even conflict. India has charged China for deliberately keeping the border issue unresolved so that it can continue to serve as a pressure point on India. Both sides after discussion have reached an understanding to exchange maps of their respective perceptions of the Line of Actual Control (LAC) in order to identify the physical extent of the disputed areas was suddenly terminated by the Chinese side without explanation. During Prime Minister Vajpayee's visit to China in 2003, India proposed a 'political solution' to the issue, to which end Special Representatives (SRs) of the two countries were nominated and given a mandate to establish a set of guidelines (which they have done) for proceeding towards resolution. The SRs have met more than dozen times without any real breakthrough.

In order that the ongoing border dispute does not hamper the relations from prospering, both sides have agreed to a hot line and a new mechanism at the Foreign Office level to contain any escalation of incidents at the border. The settlement of the border issue would open up avenues for board cooperation between the two countries.

At the political level of cooperation, India and China have set up a multi-channel and multi-level political dialogue platform, with frequent bilateral visits for in-depth discussions to resolve difficult issues and problems. On 26 September 2011, the first Sino-Indian Strategic and Economic Dialogue was launched, in which Chinese and Indian economic and foreign affairs policymakers began frank and direct discussions. Besides, leaders from both countries have frequent meetings in bilateral, regional and global forums.

On the defence and security front, both sides have developed an understanding on the need to fighting the menace of terrorism which poses a serious threat to global peace and security. Based on this, military ties between the Indian and Chinese armed forces have been building since December 2007, when India and China: Constrained Cooperation 329 the first joint counterterrorisms exercise Hand-in-Hand was held at Kunming. After the terror attack in Mumbai in November 2008, a joint military combat exercise was conducted from 6 to 14 December 2008 in Belgaum, Karnataka, which featured joint tactical manoeuvres and drills, with a 137-strong Army contingent from the 1st Company of the Infantry Battalion of the Chengdu Military Area Command and troops from the 8 Maratha Light Infantry Battalion of the Indian Army.

On the economic front, India-China trade relations have improved significantly in recent years that China has become India's largest trading partner in goods. The bilateral trade has reached over US$ 70 billion in 2011 and is expected to reach US$ 100 billion by 2015. The economic dimension of the relationship has acquired a new dynamic with the institutionalizing of a Strategic Economic Dialogue between the two countries. Besides, the two-way investment links between the two countries are also increasing. Overall, India's strategic thinkers should carefully analyse China's moves which have the potential to adversely affect India's interests and take effective steps to safeguard these interests. On the other hand, it would be in India's interest to pursue areas of mutually beneficial engagement, both in a bilateral and in a multilateral framework.

-- Dr. Sanjay Kumar

1

China - Unrest in Xinjiang: Analysis and Implications

LT GEN R.N. Singh, AVSM, SM, VSM, PVSM

Introduction

XUAR (Xinjiang Uyghur Autonomous Region) is a territory in western China that accounts for one-sixth of China's land and is home to about twenty million people from thirteen major ethnic groups, the largest of which (*more than eight million*) is the Uyghur, a predominantly Muslim community with ties to Central Asia. XUAR has remained ridden with ethnic tensions since the 1970s which stem from a deep-rooted sense of

Director General, Military Intelligence, New Delhi

alienation amongst the native Uyghur Muslims from the Han majority, the heavy-handed approach to security by Chinese authorities and a continued feeling of deprivation with regard to available social and economic opportunities. Preventing large scale social unrest anywhere in China has been one of the important domestic objectives for the Chinese government. Stability in the region continues to be one of the biggest challenges facing the Chinese leadership.

Therefore, the question in being is that - are theviolent incidents in Xinjiang a crisis of ethnicity or economy? And isthis crisis a prelude to China's bigger terrorism problem? The regions affected by terrorism and unrest in China are Xinjiang, Tibet and Inner Mongolia. A colonial impulse based on 'Han chauvinism' has prevented Beijing from effectively integrating these regions with the mainland. Particularly, Chinese authorities are also concerned about the fall-out of the post-2014 security situation in Afghanistan on XUAR. Renewed ethnic violence since July 2009, has kept the Uyghur problem on the international radar to the discomfiture of Chinese authorities. At the same time, economic imperatives demand early stabilization of the region given its vast reserves of coal and shale gas, as well as its potential as a trade and transit hub, given its location as a gateway to the West.

In view of the ideological linkages of Uyghur nationalism and alleged connections with international jihadist organisations, this chapter deliberates on the unrest in Xinjiang and delineates the trajectory of the separatist struggle and analyzes the response of the Chinese state and its future momentum.

Genesis of Terrorism in China

Xinjiang.

(a) Xinjiang which literally means '**new frontiers**' has only been a province of China since 1884, when it was annexed during the Qing dynasty. After its collapse in 1911, Xinjiang reverted to warlordism; in 1949 China regained its sway over Xinjiang. The ethnic inhabitants of Xinjiang are the Uyghurs who are concentrated in south western Xinjiang. From a being a mere 6 per cent of Xinjiang's population in 1949, the Han Chinese have risen to nearly 40 per cent of Xinjiang's population altering the demographic profile of the province.

(b) The ethnic Uyghur minority is a Turkic-speaking, predominantly Muslim community in Xinjiang abutting the Central Asian Republics, and are ethno-culturally much closer to people from across Central Asia than the Hans. The large scale migration of Hans in Xinjiang has further fuelled ethnic strains, as Uyghurs suffer owing to unemployment, expansion of Han-owned businesses and large-scale disintegration of their own culture.

(c) Religious freedom has also been a constant source of tension in Xinjiang. The Uyghurs, who look and sound more like Turks than Han Chinese, advocate and support the creation of an independent state for Xinjiang's Muslims, much to China's antagonism, leading to continued violence in the region.

Tibet

The Tibetan issue is by far the most well-known issues today. The major issues of friction were the state patronized demographic change and the increasing number of Han Chinese being relocated into Tibet. There was a lack of religious freedomwith the Chinese trying to impose themselves on the Tibetan religious ways. The consistent persecution and detention of countless monks and nuns continued as result of Chinese policies. The period from 1987 - 1993 saw major round of demonstrations and protests in Tibet; thereafter there have been no major terrorist incidents in Tibet.

Inner Mongolia

The ethnically distinct Inner Mongolians share strong cultural and historic linkages with Mongolia rather that the Chinese main land. Today the ethnic Mongolians have been relegated to abject minority and comprise approximately 17% of the total population of Inner Mongolia Autonomous Region. The grievances of the ethnic Mongolians are similar; the Chinese government consistently discriminated against the ethnic Inner Mongolians, denying them the way of nomadic life, their language, culture and enforcing forced relocations. Compared to Xingjiangand Tibet, the Chinese have been more successful in integrating Inner Mongolia into the Chinese mainstream.

Part I - Significance of Xinjiang

The Valuable Frontier

Xinjiang is the gateway between Central Asia and the East. Being situated along the fabled ancient Silk Route, it has been a prominent centre of commerce for more than 2,000 years. Since 1955, Xinjiang has been an autonomous region, Xinjiang Uighur Autonomous Region of the PRC, after briefly existing as an independent East Turkestan Republic with Soviet support. It is also sometimes referred to as Chinese Turkestan, East Turkestan or Uyghuristan, all of which denote the various perceptions of the issue. It is home to a number of Turkic ethnic groups, the largest of whom are the Uyghurs. Predominantly Sunni Muslim, they are one of China's 56 officially recognised ethnicities[1].

Xinjiang is a large, sparsely populated area, consisting of Tarim and Dzungaria regions of northwest China and spanning over 1.6 million sq km which takes up about one-sixth of the country's territory, making it the largest political sub-division of China. Xinjiang has always interested the West due to its strategic location in Inner Asia and for housing the huge Chinese nuclear testing site of Lop Nor. Closer home, the Karakoram and Xinjiang-Tibet Highways, and the Aksai Chin issue kept it in the Indian focus. The Chinese area of focus has been slightly more practical. Apart from being valuable real estate to accommodate the huge Han population, Xinjiang has large deposits of mineral and oil – this sector now accounting for 60 percent of Xinjiang's local economy[2].

Strategic Importance of XUAR

Geo Strategic Location

Chinese interest in ensuring stability of the XUAR stems not only from its paranoia about the assimilation of ethnic minorities but also from its geo-strategic location - straddling the doorway to Central Asia; its traditional utility as a buffer with the Islamic Turkic republics; and its vast potential natural resources of oil, coal and shale gas. Coal continues to provide 70% of China's energy needs and XUAR is assessed to have 2.2 trillion tonnes of coal resources; sevenshale gas basins that China has, the Tarim basin in XUAR is one of the richest. The energy resources make XUAR vital to China's future economic well-being.

Gateway to Central Asia

Xinjiang borders eight of China's neighbours in Central Asia and South Asia. Chinese sensitivities to Xinjiang also arise from three of the former Soviet Republics -Kazakhstan, Kyrgyzstan and Uzbekistan having a significant Uyghur population. Moreover, Kazakhstan continues to tacitly support the WUC. China has also been concerned about the suspected linkages of Islamic Movement of Uzbekistan (IMU), a militant organization raised in 1991, with the unrest in XUAR. Consequently, besides economic imperatives, Beijing's overtures to the CARs stem from concerns over containing the unrest in XUAR. China's annual trade with CARs, through XUAR, increased from $527 mn in 1992 to $ 46 bn in 2012. To facilitate trade, China has focused on enhancing rail and road connectivity, with the completion of a major rail link linking China-Central Asia-Europe (Zengzhou- Hamburg), a highway corridor connecting XUAR to CARs-Russia- Europe and planned oil and gas pipelines to Uzbekistan, Turkmenistan and Kazakhstan. Thus, Chinese overtures to placate CARs are evident due to its sensitivity in Xinjiang.

Part II –Reasons of Unrest and its Violent Manifestations

Growing Socio-Economic Inequalities

The active Han migration being fostered by the Government, over the years, has substantially altered the demographic balance in Xinjiang. From a population of around 3 mn Uighurs, and 2.22 lakh Hans, in the late 1940s, recent figures indicate only a small difference with 9.41mn Uighurs and 8.12 mn Hans[3]. There is also a sharp difference in income levels, with a 2009 analysis indicating that while the average annual income in Southern Xinjiang (where Uighurs are in majority) was 3,142 Yuan, the average rural income in Northern parts of Xinjiang (Hans dominated) was over three times this figure. Uyghurs comprise only around 9% of the total work force in XUAR and even seasonal agricultural labour is hired from other provinces. The language barrier further prevents ethnic Uyghurs from availing the educational and employment benefits that the State has to offer, leading to socio – economic inequalities.

Religious Persecution in XUAR

Given the growth of religious extremism in some of the neighbouring countries, China has been imposing restrictions on religious activities even during the month of 'Ramzan'. Many of these restrictions are in keeping with an official pledge by XUAR authorities to crackdown against what they term as "illegal religious activities". Religious affairs bureaus of the Government andcommittees of the CCP have the power to register and supervise all religious organisations, sites, clerics and inspect activities being conducted therein. Curbs instituted periodically, by the Government in Xinjiang, include preventing children from observing Ramzan, from entering mosques and to resolutely opposing their fasting. Supervision of mosques and religious places generally increases all-over Xinjiang during the holy month.

The Islamic Uyghurs in Xinjiang and Policies of the CCP

Islam has had a presence in China almost since its birth and is most evident in thenorthwest of the country, especially in Xinjiang, which borders Central Asia. The Turkic peoples, of whom the Uyghurs are an important constituent, were Islamised inthe 10th century. The strength of Islamic culture varies enormously amongst Muslims in China – whilst the Hui of Fujian have beenmuch more relaxed about their Islamic identity and are traditionally loyal to the Chinese state, the Uyghur Muslims adhere fiercely to the traditional Islamic culture[4]. This is probably why the CCP adopted such harsh policies towards Uyghur Muslims. Muslim grievances have largely been due to the official maltreatment of their community.

During the 18th and 19th century, when Muslims inboth the north-west and south-west of China rebelled, they were severely crushed. Under Communist rule, observance of Islamic rules and customs became even harder[5]. During the

Cultural Revolution (1966–1976), all religious activities and organisations went underground; gross violations of human rights were perpetrated in Xinjiang, with the international community being kept in the dark. In March, 1996, the CCP in its Document 7 directed the local authorities in Xinjiang to take firmer action tostop the burgeoning threat of ethnic separatism and conflict[6]. It charged that groups were fomenting trouble, indulging inbombing and committing terrorist attacks and claimed that the chaos and turmoil, if not checked, would affect stability in Xinjiang and eventually the whole country.

Ethnicity As Lynchpin

As a multi ethnic state, China grapples with the question of balancing indigenous cultural development with foreign influences. While Hansare the majority community in China, in Xinjiang, Uyghurs constitute the largerethnic group. The 'peaceful liberation' of Xinjiang in1949 is seen as a sham by Uyghurs in retrospect. The main factor thus, leading to antithetical perceptions amongst the Uyghur and Han communities is the *abandonment* of theassurance of religious and cultural autonomy, which was promised by the PRC in the early 1950s but given up formaking Xinjiang an "inseparable" part ofChina.

In the present scenario, the rapid pacewith which China is allowing Han population to settle in the region has become a significant cause of discontentamong the Uyghurs. They vehemently resent ethnic based discrimination policies and believe that these are heavily biased in favour of Hans: Ethnic discrimination by the state is palpable even at mundane levels of health amenities which fuels a discourse of deprivation amongst Uyghurs[7].

Policies in Xinjiang - Similar to Tibet

The use of coercion is not uncommon in Chinese

history as far as religious groups are concerned. Policies towards Xinjiang are similar to the policies that were directed towards Tibet. As far as Tibetan Buddhism is concerned, moves against the Dalai Lama were accompanied by a series of 'patriotic education campaigns', which aimed to win over support to the Chinese among ordinary Tibetans. China launched a campaign to fully integrate Tibet into the PRC politicallyand socially and militarily[8]. In places like Tibet, in a visible show of force, the Chinese began entrenching their troops around the buildings they had occupied during the Tibetan invasion, and imposed tighter control over religious life.

Whilst, Tibet has been forcefully annexed due to its predominant non – violent opposition led by HE Dalai Lama and sparse population; Xinjiang would continue to pose a security threat due to itsproximity to a Muslim neighbourhood and its geo – strategic location – bridge between the East and Central Asia.

Part III - Separatism or Terrorism

Rise of Uyghur Nationalism

The recent emergence of the Xinjiang issue is an indicator of gradual but steady Islamic reassertion in Central Asia. Authors like Andrew Forbes have also analysed the rise of Pan-Turkism, the theory that all of the Turkish speaking societies, from Turkey, through Central Asia to Xinjiang were likely to emergein a political alliance, and concluded that this Islamic reassertion is part of this Pan-Turkism. However, prior to the 20th century, the cities of East Turkestan, hosting Turkic ethnicities such as Uyghurs, Kyrgyz, Uzbeks, Kazakhs and Tajiks,held little unified nationalistic identity. Under Qing and later ROC rule, a largely Uyghur-based identity began toform. The short lived East Turkestan Republics further fuelled the Uyghur hopes and nationalist aspirations. It is commonly believed that during China's Civil War, the Communists had promised Tibet and Xinjiang a federation of republics. Mao later reneged on this and instead introduced his notion of "autonomous" regions, provinces and districts[9]. This poor substitution obviously did not satisfy the Tibetans and the Uyghurs, and the Communists had a difficult time in controlling both these "autonomous" lands.

After the declarations of independence in the erstwhile Soviet republics of Kazakhstan, Kyrgyzstan, Tajikistan, Turkmenistan and Uzbekistan from the Soviet Union in 1991 (these republics ethnically are often called West Turkestan or Russian Turkestan), the calls for the liberation of East Turkestan (or XUAR) from China began to surface again. Initially, the Hans were forcibly relocated to Xinjiang, but the later migrations were mainly due to the economic incentives provided by the Chinese government and the activities of the Xinjiang Production and Construction Corps (XPCC), a semi military organisation of settlers that built farms, towns, and cities overscattered parts of Xinjiang[10].

Separatism Or Terrorism

Violent incidents in Xinjiang have been dubbed interchangeably as 'separatist' and 'terrorist' acts orchestrated by Uyghur elements basedabroad (for instance, organizations like the ETIM), orby prominent Uyghurs like Rebiya Kadeer. Analysis of the larger geopolitical situation reveals thatwhile separatist tendencies have beenbolstered by religious repression and lack of economic benefits, there are several external factors charting the blueprint of China's national and regional polities. Most notably, Soviet influence in Xinjiang hindered initial assimilation with the People's Republic of China (PRC) during early twentieth century, while the Islamic extremist linkages with the Central Asian region have been responsible for undercutting the state's authority in the late twentieth century. Consequently, China has been continuously engaged in an endeavour to eliminate the Islamic threat through confidence building measures with its neighbouring countries.

The international recognition to violence in Xinjiang is accrued more in terms of safeguarding human rights and struggle of thelocal minorities against the policies of the statethan to support the separatist goals of Uyghursin Xinjiang. Given the recurrent nature of Xinjiang's separatist struggle it has established a legitimate concern for the authorities in Beijing.

The 2009 Riots

It is widely perceived that the 2009 riots, the biggest acts of violence in Xinjiang, might have been caused by a combination of economic factors and the prevalent stereotypes being sustained by the anti-terrorism campaign. Using China's integration and employment opportunities, by mid 2007, about 900,000 Uyghurs had takenup jobs outside Xinjiang[11]. Most of them were employed in semi-skilled and unskilled jobs. In doing so, they also tended to compete with their Han counterparts who flocked to China's industrial boomtowns. In the case of the Shaoguan factory, there was evidence to show that a retrenched Han employee might have deliberately created an impression that the Uyghur workers hadraped two Han women. This led to subsequent bloody clash in the factory as well as inside the dormitories. After the government repressed the news about the truth about the Shaoguan factory incident, it escalated intoa much bigger and bloodier clash in Kashgar on the 5/6 of July in which nearly 200 people (largely Hans) were killed[12]. It highlighted the issue that co-employment was not a solution to ethnic integration unless concerted efforts aimed at ethnic sensitisation were in place.

After the outbreak of fresh violence in mid-2011 and more recently in February 2012, China finds itself at a crossroads; stricter control seems to be backfiring politically where as development isfurther raising inequality instead of controlling it. While one may not see escalated violencein the future, it can be concluded that the unintended consequences of state policy areleading to a situation whereby the state is not sure as to what it can do in the future.

International Terrorism and Violence Profile

The violent chapter of the Uighur nationalist movement is spearheaded by the East Turkistan Islamic Movement (ETIM). The movement was founded in 1993 in Hotan, XUAR and emerged as a cohesive movement in 1997, after its leader, Hasan Mahsum, moved the ETIM headquarters to Kabul, in Taliban-controlled Afghanistan. The ETIM was invigorated by the success of the Afghan Jehad with the Taliban, in the 1990s, giving sanctuary and support to Central Asian Islamic militant groups, even as their alliance with the al-Qaeda deepened. The military capabilities of the ETIM were, however, degraded after the US invasion of Afghanistan. Thereafter, open inputs indicated that the ETIM may have metamorphed into the Turkistan Islamic Party (TIP). The TIP/ETIM gained some publicity during attacks orchestrated in Xinjiang province prior to the Beijing Olympics (August 2008).

Currently, the TIP/ETIM professes that its primary goal is to liberate Xinjiang from Chinese control. It is allied with the Taliban and has been listed as a terrorist organization by the UN since 2002. The ETIM is reported to have strength of around 200 cadres within XUAR. Chinese authorities, however, continue to attribute most of the violent incidents in XUAR to the ETIM.

The Af-Pak region has been a major recruiting, training and motivating ground for terrorists of all hues including Uyghur extremists, and Beijing remains concerned that the ETIM continues to secure sustenance and succour in the region. It has been raising the issue with Pakistan and the role of Pakistani groups in terrorist activities in XUAR. The JuD/LeT was cited as one of the groups assisting the Uyghur militants. The activities of ETIM remain one of the important issues of concern in the otherwise 'all/ weather friendship' discourse that characterizes the Sino-Pakistan relations. China fears that terrorist groups may re-establish safe havens in Afghanistan after 2014 and is keen to ensure that security mechanism in place is capable of dealing with such threats. In addition, China is also concerned about the possible threat such extremists could pose to its growing economic interests in Afghanistan.

Violence profile since 2001 and the various terrorist organisations prevalent in the region are enumerated at Appendices A and B.

Part IV - State Response

State Policy on Xinjiang

In the first three decades after 'liberation', the major focus of the Chinese government's Xinjiang policy was establishing control. One of the prominent methods by which itattempted this was by encouraging Han Chinese migration into Xinjiang. Thus, with development came the Han migrants but over a period of time they substantially altered the demographic structure of the province and also exacerbated the feeling of deprivation amongst the Uyghurs. During this period, the government also focused upon reducing the influence of Islam in the region[13]. In addition, excessive damage was doneduring the years of Cultural Revolution when, in the name of 'eliminating the old', a lotof the cultural heritage of the minorities was destroyed.

In order to address these tensions, the Chinese government initiated a softer and inclusive approach after 1985 when affirmative action, economic development and recognition ofthe Uyghur's different identity became a part of policy[14]. In addition, increased extraction of energy resources in Xinjiang, created a feeling that the state was exploiting the province for the growth elsewhere. Subsequently, violence raised its head in Xinjiang in the 1990s when thes eparatists were reinvigorated following the creation of Central Asian states based on ethnic identities after the disintegration of the Soviet Union. This in turn led to the renewalof China's hardliner approach aimed at rooting out 'the three evils' ofterrorism, separatism and religious extremism'. Termed by state agencies as "Strike hard/maximum pressure!" this approach had its roots in Beijing's fears about Uyghur separatiststrying to emulate the example of the Central Asian states and pushing for liberation. Thus, the hardliner approach was followed alongside economic development policy, a form of incentive for peace.

China's Counter Terrorist Policies

China's initial actions to curb violence in Xinjiang were brutal; there were wide scale reports of security-force excesses and torture. However, limited success forced China to reduce brutality of its repression and pulled the military out of direct confrontation with society. It builtmore restrained, effective and specialized police forces and reinvigorated political and educational projects in Xinjiang. The Chinese counter terrorist policies were a mix of "hard and soft" strategy. Whilst, hard measures were introduced to clamp down on dissidents advocating independence or self-determination through elections, thesoft measures attempted to win over support, or at least acquiescence, of the minorities and its minority policies. The four major aspects of this strategy were crushing separatism, promoting economic development, distinguishing non-separatist from separatist demands and expanding personal liberties.

Scenario Post 2009 Riots

The Chinese government responded to the 2009 riots

in two ways: at political level, it fixed accountability for the riots; and, second, at economic level, it create deconomic incentives to foster peace.

Political Reshuffle. Changes effectedat the political level aimed at changing the popular perception about the Party. The CPC appointed Zhang Chunxian, asoft liner as the Xinjiang Party Secretary, in place of Wang Lequan, a hardliner who was credited with promoting the stability first policy and enforcing it in a strict manner[15]. However, recurrence of violence showed that leadership change at the provincial level did little to restore the faith about the Party-State amongst the aggrieved Uyghurs.

Economic Incentives. Major economic initiatives were undertaken for improving theeconomic conditions of the Uyghurs,with overarching goals of 'leapfrog development' and 'promot estability'[16]:-

- Government investment was to double to almost two trillion Yuan.
- Reforms to peg tax on the prices of oil and gas, which allowed the locals the benefits of increased oil and gas prices around the world; this resulted in $615-$700 million in profits.
- A system of pairing assistance, where 19 richer provinces and cities would contribute a% of their GDP to·the pair region.
- Special economic zones established at Kashgar, Alataw and Korgas.

China's Strike Hard Campaigns: Curbing Separatism?

In 1996, the Chinese government initiated the 'Strike Hard Campaigns' as one of the principal tools of weeding out alleged impertinent elements. This was carried out by tightly observing religious activities and festivals, monitoring Muslims who had returned from studying in the madrasas of Pakistan and the Middle East, arresting and executing suspected terrorists, indicting known separatists, establishing a number of anti-terrorist surveillance centres and quick reaction units in sensitive regions. The strike hard campaigns manifested asacts of suppression of religious and individual rights in the Xinjiang province. The government's efforts in Xinjiang hereafter were based on itspolicy of Han in-migration, exploitation of Xinjiang's potential energy resources andgreater political and economic links with Central Asia[17]. The Strike Hard Campaigns fomented more distrust between the locals and the state and consequently came to be abhorred by the indigenous minorities. The inefficacy of these repressive measures forced the Chinese authorities to adopt newer methods to assuage the Uyghurs.

Part V –Way Ahead

Looking Ahead

The unrest in Xinjiang has seen the greatest political loss of life in China since the Tiananmen massacre in 1989. In addition, because of the political sensitivities surrounding China's treatment of its Muslim community, China is also worried that the recent crisis is likely to tarnish its reputationin the Middle East and the greater Islamic world, and perhaps endanger its energy security prospects. The majority of Uyghurs are still moderates as radicalisation is only in itsnascent stages and the influence of terror groups still on the remote fringes. Most of them would settle for genuine autonomy rather than an independent East Turkestan, much to China's liking.

If the Chinese leadership continues to opt for the iron fist, the majority of Uyghurs who clearly favour non-violent means to attain a higher degreeof autonomy and not independence, might be turned into implacable foes of what they perceive as chauvinistic Han-Chinese colonisers. But such a pragmatic analysis seems unlikely in Beijing in the near future as the Communists are buoyed by the success of Sinification in Inner Mongolia and Manchuria, and willpush the immigration-driven Sinification in Xinjiang beyond the half-way homepoint.

Unresolved Structural Problems

Measures by Government has done little to correct the causes of economic concern and socio-economic inequality prevalent in Xinjiang. It is unlikely that China would be able to resolve these problems anytime soonor reversing the policies of the last 60 years. Four important areas ofsocio-economic concerns to demonstrate this argument are:-

(a) **Migration.** The increasing ratio of the Han population has made the Uyghurs strangers in their own land.[18] *Table 1* illustrates the massive influx of migrants over the last 50 years.

	1945	1982	1996	2002	2006
Uyghur	2,988,528	5,995,947	7,916,013	8,692,300	9,413,796
Han	222,401	5,283,971	6,432,816	7,595,700	8,121,588
% of Minorities	**93.85**	59.73	61.92	60.13	**57.40**

Table 1: Demographic Profile of Xinjiang in Some Selected Years[19]

(b) **Intra-regional Inequality**. The relative semblance of economic prosperity hides a deeper intra-regional disparity, which, is a major cause of Uighur resentment against Chinese policies. It is observed that the southern areas are generally impoverished unlike the developed parts of northern Xinjiang which tend to attract Han settlers and which are managed by the Xinjiang Production and Construction Corps (XPCC).[20]

(c) **Unemployment**. The XPCC-led development has concentrated in the north (Han dominated), again increasing the perception that state support is largely usurped by the Han migrants. Due to lack of fluency in

Mandarin and technical skills, Uyghurs find themselves disadvantaged at finding jobs in either state or private enterprises and increasing the local unemployment.

(d) **Education**. Economic inequalities are also exacerbated by unequal access to education. Although theoretically the Uyghurs are supposed to enjoy quotas and other preferential policies to ensure better education and job opportunities, in practice the partial withdrawal of state financing in these sectors has led to an increase n the cost of education, thereby reducing the number of people who can afford to send their children to school.

Strategic Implications

China's foreign policy behaviour with regards to its Xinjiang quandary reflects three major concerns. First, the increasing demand for transparent governments in Central Asia could have a threatenings pillover effect in Xinjiang as it could leadto further radicalization of Uyghur separatists. Second, due to the large Uyghur presence in neighbouring countries, there could bea potential terrorist risk to the vast network of expansive infrastructure (eg, road, railway, pipeline). Third, the ties with the neighbouring countries in terms of Islam could promote further secessionist tendencies.

China's interactions with its southern neighbours, India and Pakistan, are also arranged within the ambit of containing terrorism in this region. However, China continues to have difficulties with Pakistan on the issue of the latter's ability to crack down on terrorism aimed at China[21]. In this context, Xinjiang's ties with Indiaare important. In the security realm, the eastern part of Ladakh which is the disputed Aksai Chin area that China occupied in the 1962 war and through which it had built a road in the early 1950s to logistically connect Tibet[22] needs to be taken into account. China's vulnerability and need for stability in the region could help India find an opening in improving relations with China.

It should be recognized that the manner in which China deals with Xinjiang's ethnic and terrorist threats would affectthe larger context of Asian security environment. On the one hand, China's strategy in Xinjiang and Central Asia could place within its grasp an unprecedented opportunity to extend its power and influence into the Central Asian region. On the other hand, it holds the potential to destabilize the entire Chinese state. There is some speculation that any mishandling of the Xinjiang question could lead to break up of China in amanner similar to USSR. And since most of the infrastructure and energy projects are grounded in this region, any disturbance in the area couldcreate potential havoc for the Chinese economy, which it can ill afford at this juncture[23].

Conclusion

Given the larger geostrategic importance of the region, it is imperative that China finds a lasting solution to its Uyghur problem. The Urumqi crisis of 2009 is only one such violent manifestation of there sentment caused by the misinterpretation of local cultural and political desires. Though the massive derailment of its peace initiative in the region should have led to a reassessment of its policies, post Urumqi developments do not reflect a serious appraisal by the Chinese government. In continuing with its repressive policies, the government is yet again perpetrating a legitimacy crisisfor itself and adding fuel to the disgruntlement of the Uyghurs. Prioritizing one facet over the other will not provide any lasting solutions to the current situation in Xinjiang; development based singularly on an economic agenda or only in tune with the ethnic aspirations would only intensify the cleavage between the haves and havenots. There is a pressing need for shifting the discourse from that of 'controlling Xinjiang' to that of 'accommodating Xinjiang'.

The 2009 riots occurred as a consequence of the deep-rooted ethnic biases prevalent in Chinese society, coupled with the state's hard handed approach and the sense of deprivation among Uyghurs. Perceptive to the problem and alert to the situation, the Chinese government as introduced more economic incentives for the local population. However, the deeprooted causes of the tension remain unresolved and repeated instances of violence only indicate that some of the policies may be backfiring.

To help Sinicise the Western regions, Beijing has evolved a five pronged strategy cartographically altering ethnic-homeland boundaries, demographically flooding non-Han cultures, rewriting history to justify Chinese control, enforcing cultural homogeneity to held blur local identities, and maintaining political repression. With Manchu assimilated into Han society and the swamping of the locals in Inner Mongolia has left only the Tibetans and the Turkic-speaking Uyghurs as the holdouts. These traditional ethnic minority lands have become the country's Achilles' heel. The modifying factors in such occurrence will be the states' approach towards the minorities, the unaddressed minorities grievances, the global human rights agenda and the support to the cause of Uyghur and Tibetans from around the world.

Beijing's development policies in Xinjiang need to be more balanced, respecting the cultural traditions of the Uyghurs with equitable distribution of the national income. Unemployment must be addressed through targeted programmes that increase Uyghur employment and implement policies that raise their economic standards in rural areas. Uyghurs and Hans also need to understand each other's perspective. As the majority group in China, the Hans bear a greater responsibility for maintaining positive ethnic relations and trustneeds to be built through constructive dialogue. This task is trickier in the case of Xinjiang because not only is it plagued by the general set of problems prevalent elsewhere in China like socio-economic inequality, human rights violations, strict media control, etc, but its geographic location, economic status, the ethnic identity of its people and their aspirations and linkages with people across the border, all add layers of complexity andare a cause of worryfor the Chinese leadership.

Appendix A

(Refers to Para 28)

Violence Profile : Xinjiang Province

Yr	Loc	Incident
2001	Kashgar	Assassination of PRC officials on 03 Feb 2001
2002	Bishkek	Chinese diplomat and driver killed
2003	Bishkek	Ldr of Uyghur community killed
2003	Urumqi	Bus hijacking on 27 Mar 2003. 22 Killed
2005	Turpan	Two people killed - crackdown on Uyghur protestors
2007	Pamir	Raid by Chinese tps on trt camp in Jn 2007. 18 killed
2008	Kashgar	17 police offrs and border troops killed
2008	Kuqa	10 attackers & 01 security guard killed in bombings
2009	**Urumqi**	**Riots on 05-07 Jul 2009. Nearly 200 dead**
2009	Urumqi	Riots on 02 Sep 2009. 75 persons were arrested.
2010	Aksu	07 Killed when 03 Uyghurs rammed explosive laden tri cycle into Police Patrol- Aug 2010
2011	Kashgar	13 Han Chinese killed in terrorist strike - 31 Jul
2011	Kashgar	13 killed and 27 injured on 30-31 Jul 2011.
2011	Hotan	Police kill 20 protestors on 18 Jul 2011
2011	Pishan	Police kill 07 trts on 28 Dec 2011
2012	Yecheng	Rioters armed with knives kill 10 persons- Feb 2012
2013	Kashgar	21 killed incl 15 Police/Govt officials - 21 Apr 13
2013	Kashgar	19 convicted of extremist crimes on 20 Jun 2013
2013	Turpan	27 killed in riots - Jun 2013
2013	Maralbexi	Riots; 15 persons killed.
2013	Turpan	PRO Govt Imam killed
2013	Aksu	Riots; 03 persons killed
2013	Kargilik	Separatist violence. 22 were killed.

Appendix B

(Refers to Para 28)

Terrorist Organisations : Xinjiang

1. **ETIM.**
   (a) Islamist Extremist Group.
   (b) Movement for creating an Islamist state.
   (c) Taliban support and funding from Al-Qaeda.
   (d) Other funding sources-org crime, drug trafficking, arms smuggling, kidnapping and extortion.
   (e) Criminals and militants who have fled China.

2. **ETLO (East Turkestan Liberation Org).**
   (a) Better known as Shat.
   (b) Oppose Hans in Xinjiang and achieve independence.
   (c) Series of politically motivated bombings and armed attacks.
   (d) Use of chemical in attacks.

3. **Other Militant Orgs.**
   (a) Home of East Turkistan youth.
   (b) Eastern Turkistan Liberation Front (Sharki Turkistan Azatlik Front).
   (c) Free Turkistan movement.
   (d) Eastern Turkistan (Sharki Turkistan)Revolutionary Party.
   (e) Eastern Turkistan Indep Org (Sharki Turkistan Azatlik Teshkilati).
   (f) Eastern Turkistan(Sharki Turkistan) Islamic Party.
   (g) Islamic Holy Warriors.
   (h) Eastern Turkistan Grey Wolf Party (Sharki Turkistan Bozkurt Party).

4. Uyghur Org : Outside Xinjiang.

(a) Committee For Eastern Turkistan - Kazakhstan

(b) United National Revolutionary Front Of East Turkistan - Kazakhstan

(c) Xinjiang Liberation Organization/Uyghur Liberation Organization (ULO) – Tajikstan & Kyrgyzstan

(d) Islamic Movement of Uzbekistan (IMU)

5. Organisations Active on the Internet.

(a) East Turkistan Information Centre.

(b) World Uyghur Youth Congress.

(c) East Turkistan National Congress.

(d) Uyghur American Association.

Bibliography

1. Shailendra Arya, 'Xinjiang: China's Fourth Frontier', CLAWS Journal, Summer 2010.
2. Avinash Godbole and Akash Goud, 'China's Xinjiang Problem: The 2009 Riots and its aftermath', IDSA Issue Brief, Apr 20112.
3. Bhavna Singh, 'Ethnicity, Separatism and Terrorism in Xinjiang', Institute of Peace and Conflict Studies, Aug 2010.
4. Kunal Mukherjee, 'The Uyghur Question in Contemporary China', Strategic Analysis, May 2010.
5. Amnesty International Report, People's Republic of China: China's Anti-Terrorism Legislation and Repression In the Xinjiang Uyghur Autonomous Region, March 22, 2002, *http:/ /web.amnesty.org/ library.*
6. Andrews, Martin, Beijing's Growing Security Dilemma in Xinjiang, China Brief, Volume: 5, Issue: 13, December 2011.
7. Clarke Michael, China's 'War On Terror' in Xinjiang: Human security and the Causes of Uyghur Separatism, Terrorism and Violence, Vol. 20.

8. Chaudhuri, Debasish, Survey of Economic Situation in Xinjiang and its Role in Twenty-First Century, China Report, Vol.41, No.1, Jan-Mar 20.

9. Davis, Elizabeth Van Wie, Uyghur Muslim Separatism in Xinjiang, China, Asia- Pacific Centre for Security Studies, January 2008.

10. Mackerras, Colin, 'Xinjiang at the Turn of the Century: The Causes of Separatism', Central Asian Survey, Vol. 20, No.3, Sept 2001.

11. White Paper on the History and Development of Xinjiang, 2003, Online web URL: *http://www.gov.cn/english/official/2005-07/28/ content_17948.* htm.

12. Starr, Frederick S (ed.), Xinjiang: China's Muslim Borderland, M E Sharpe, Armonk, New York, London, England, 2004.

13. Zang, Xiaowei, Minority Ethnicity, Social Status and Uyghur Involvement in Urban Xinjiang, Asian Ethnicity, Vol.8, No.1, Feb 2007.

14. J. Millward, 'Violent Separatism in Xinjiang: A Critical Assessment', *Policy Studies 6*, East– West Centre, Washington, DC, 2004.

15. A. T. Grunfeld, *The Making of Modern Tibet*, M. E. Sharpe, New York and Armonk, London,1996.

16. Monika Chansoria, 'China Keeps Close Guard on restive Xinjiang', Article No 1795, CLAWS Journal, 04 Apr 11.

References

1. Shailendra Arya, '*Xinjiang: China*'s fourth frontier', CLAWS Journal, Summer 2010; pg 189.

2. Ibid; pg 189.

3. Monika Chansoria, '*China keepsclose guard on restive Xinjiang*', Article No 1795, CLAWS Journal, 04 Apr 11.

4. C. Mackerras, '*China*'s Ethnic Minorities and Globalisation,' No. 20, pg 119.

5. Ibid, pg 182-183.
6. Ibid, pg 52.
7. Brenda L. Schuster, 'Gaps in the Silk Road: An analysis of the population health disparities in the XUAR,' The China Quarterly, 198, (June 2009).
8. A T Grunfeld, '*The Making of Modern Tibet*', M. E. Sharpe, New York and Armonk, London, 1996.
9. Subroto Roy, '*China*'s India Example: Tibet, Xinjiang may not be Assimilated like Inner Mongolia and Manchuria, '*The Statesman*, Editorial Page Special Article, March 25,2008, *www.thestatesman.net*.
10. Shailendra Arya, 'Xinjiang: China's fourth frontier',. CLAWS Journal, Summer 2010; pg 195.
11. James Millward, "Introduction: does the 2009 Urumchi violence mark a turning point?", Central Asian Survey 28 (4), December 2009, pg 351.
12. Ibid; pg 351.
13. Anthony Howell, '*Population Migration and Labor Market Segmentation: Empirical Evidence from Xinjiang,Northwest China*', Masters Thesis, Michigan State University, pg 31, 2009.
14. S. Frederick Starr, 'China's Changing Strategic Concerns: Impact on Human Rights in Xinjiang', 16 Nov 05.
15. Shan Wei & Weng Cuifen, '*China*'s New Policy in Xinjiang and its Challenges', East Asian Policy, July/Sep 2010, pg 61.
16. '*Xinjiang*'s economy set to be transformed', People's Daily Online (English), September 9, 2010.
17. Clarke Michael, '*China*'s 'war on terror' in Xinjiang', Vol.20, No.2, pg 261-289.
18. World Uyghur Congress, '*One Year after the Xinjiang Work Conference: Ethnic Division and Inequality Remain Unchanged in East Turkestan*', Press Release of 20 May 2011.

19. Debashish Chauduri, *'Minority Economy in Xinjiang'*, China Report, Feb 2010, Vol. 46, No. 1, pg 14.

20. White paper on Xinjiang, *'History and Development of Xinjiang'*, Chapter IX, "Xinjiang production and construction corps", 2003.

21. Ziad Haider, *'Clearing clouds over Karakoram, 'Daily Times*, 4 April 2004.

22. Abanti Bhattacharya, *'Xinjiang*'s governor's visit to India: Significance for China- India Relations'; http:*//www.ipcs.org/article/china/xinjiangsgovernors-visit-to-india-significance-for-indiachina-relations-1546.html.*

23. Yuchao Zhu and Dongyan Blachford, 'China's fate as a Multinational state: a preliminary assessment,' Journal of Contemporary China, 15(47), May 2006, pg 329.

2

Impact of India – China Relations on Future World System

Dr. Babita Maji

Introduction

Now the growing perception is that the global economic gravity has shifted to Asia towards India and China, the emerging economic power houses in the region will shape the 21st century. In making such feelings a reality however, the nature of the future dynamics of domestic condition as well as external relations of the two nations appears a crucial factor. New Delhi and Beijing have established a strategic and cooperative partnership for peace and prosperity and signed a document on shared vision for the 21st century signifying that the Sino-Indian ties have gone beyond the bilateral context and acquired a global character.[1] The point has been mentioned that the India-China relationship is essentially bilateral in nature, but the relationship has also been shaped and conditioned, by the

Assistant Professor, Department of Political Science, R.G.(P.G.) College, Meerut Email: *majibabita225@gmail.com* evolving global setting. The role of United States, only superpower in the post cold war and other major powers such as Russia, European Union and their relations with both nations also influenced the India-China interaction. Therefore, the evolving global setting and international aspects assumes importance in the comprehensive study of India-China interaction. As Therese Delpech has noted that "future relations between China and India, the world's two most populous nations are critical both to Asian, and global security.[2]

The sustained growth and fast economic development of India and China have increased their global profile which helps to play an important role for folding the structure of new world order. There is a general expectation that these two countries of South would be among those that shape the geopolitics of the rest of the century and would play a pivotal role in the restructure of global order. India and China are emerging as evolving balance of power in Asia. The concurrent economic rise of these two Asian powers implies that the next few decades will witness a massive redistribution of global wealth and power towards the eastern hemisphere. In 21st Century Jim O'Neill was pointed out that high growth rates, economic potential and demographic development were going to put BRIC further in a lead position and it was argued that their increased relevance should also be reflected in their incorporation to the G7.[3] India and China as the biggest two developing countries of BRICS play important roles in boosting Asian and global economic growth and enhancing multilateralism in international affairs. Therefore, the complexity of India's and China's rise as Asian and global powers and their complex bilateral relations are a matter of grave concern not only for the sustainability of BRICS, but also to the vision and dialogue of a multipolar world order.[4] While in 2007 the two economics accounted for only around 7% of absolute global output, if current rates of growth are sustained by both, they will resume their historic place in the next few decades. This forecast is underscored by the renewed dedication of India and China to economic rejuvenation.[5] Given this incessant shift in the international political economy, it is inevitable that Sino Indian relations would influence political economic stability in Asia, and therefore, in the international system as a whole.

During the global economic crisis of 2008 India and China were not affected as much as America and western countries. Chinese Premier Wen Jiabao stated that "what we can do now to maintain the steady and fast growth of national economy andensure that no major fluctuations will happen. That will be our great contribution to world economy for recovering the reccssion."[6] Its impact on Indian economy also was less due to lower dependence of economy on export markets and sizeable contribution to GDP is from domestic sources. Now during the Covid-19 pandemic India revisit the idea of self-reliance Bharat which help to compete and betterment innovation of domestic economy.

With the decline of US-hegemonic power, many believe that the rise of BRICS forum will contribute to promote the new multipolar world and may be prompt to a 'non-western order' in the future. As the two biggest Asian countries, India and China play important roles in boosting Asian and global economic growth and enhancing multilateralism in international affairs. The idea of BRICS was first introduce by economists of Goldman Sachs as part of economic model exercise to forecast global economic trends over the next half century. As so far, BRICS forum has held eleven summits, and we can conclude from their agendas that they are committed to the multilateralism world order and global governance as shown below: BRICS Summit (2009-2016)

Year	Location	Main Agenda
June 16, 2009	Yekaterinburg	Economic crisis, G-20 and the reform of the global financial system
April 16, 2010	Brasilia	Reform of the global financial system and the UN development and climate change
April 14, 2011	Sanya	Board range of global affairs
March 29, 2012	New Delhi	Global stability, security and prosperity, middle east and north America and climate change
March 26-27, 2013	Durban	Economic cooperation
July 14-16, 2014	Fortaleza and Brasilia	New development bank
July 8-9, 2015	Ufa	NDB and BRICS contigent reserve arrangement
October15-16, 2016	Goa	Consolidating the grouping
September3-5,2017	Xiamen	BRICS: Stronger partnership for brighter future
July25-27, 2018	Johannesburg	Collaboration for inclusive growth and shared prosperity
November13-14, 2019	Brasilia	Economic Growth for an innovative future

With the BRICS grouping emerging as the new centre of power factors in global politics, they have been the core concern in 'representation of southern values and interests' in various global multilateral forums and financial institutions.[7] The expressions 'multilateralism' and 'multi-polarism' bring new insights in the context of the rise of BRICS.[8]BRICS provides an opportunity to India to realize their dream of regional and world political power such as in the global financial bodies, climate change dialogue and negotiations. Besides, the cooperation mechanism of BRICS countries also will help India from abide by the rules to the rules makers.[9] in a globalized world politics; BRICS serves the Chinese global agenda of sidelining the western and in the progressive agenda of G-20. China has always asked for a greater role for G-20 in world politics. With the lead of

BRICS, developing powers have consistently argued that the current structure of the global financial and multilateral bodies needs to be reformed to be egalitarian and transparent.[10] India and China are committed to boost their political relations at regional and international levels such as the UN, IMF, international climate change, ASEAN regional forum and Shanghai cooperation organization. In BRICS system, China and India will greatly improve their cooperation reducing their conflicts and competition, however, India will still consider the US as the most important partner in Asia-Pacific area due to the current situation.

Now 'Indo-Pacific' is the new emerging geostrategic and geo-economic centre of the world politics that encompasses both the Indian and Pacific oceans, defined in large part by the geographically expanding interests and reach of 'emerging powers'— India and China, and the continued strategic role and presence of the 'predominant power'— United States. Therefore, there are significant regional security convergences and different degrees of strategic balancing between these major players in Indo-Pacific region, which will definitely rise rivalry between US, India and China to build a new global order. Actually, the Indo-Pacific region is a critical part of the global commons––with the United States, India and China all active there.[11] Thus, it is the most strategically contested area in the world, where both cooperation and competition simultaneously occur. China's intervention in South China Sea, OBOR, String of Pearls strategy is directly challenges to US to hegemonic stance. India's role in the Indo-Pacific is considered crucial by countries such as Australia, Japan, and the United States. It incubates a new world order with evident signals for a radical shift in international power equations. These developments in the Asia-Pacific and the growing companionship between India and the US have caught attention across the globe. The unprecedented rise of China could be the result of the strategic convergence between India and the US.[12]

Former US President Barack Obama's Rebalancing Asia Strategy focus on the security and the prosperity and the dignity of people across this region expand by The U.S. President Donald Trump as "Indo-Pacific strategy". China's rapid industrial growth made it an ideal partner for Russia, which is rich in natural resources. At present due to US-China trade war China and Russia are increasing their trade in domestic currency instead of Dollar which creat a new financial strategy. It has now become a challenge to the countries in the region including India. Concern about China's rising economic and military posturing in the region India has been an advocate to "Free and Open Indo-Pacific"[13] policy and co-operates with the U.S., Japan and Australia in combating for free and open trade in the region.

Indian Prime Minister Narendra Modi said in17th Asia Security Summit in 2018 that India's policy perspective on Indo-Pacific included "inclusiveness", "openness", "ASEAN centrality" and that the concept was not directed against any country.[14] The Indian government has introduced the concept of "SAGAR" (Security And Growth for All in the Region) and believes in an Indo-Pacific that is free, open and inclusive, and one that is founded upon a cooperative and collaborative rules-based order. Another important aspect to touch upon is the shift from India's Look East Policy to Act East Policy. India's need to access the South and East China Seas becomes important for it to trade with countries like Russia which is in the far east of India.[15] India is considered as an important geostrategic partner of the US in its Asia rebalancing and the increasing use of the term "Indo-Pacific" symbolizes it. There has been a greater co-operation between the two countries on defence and socio-economic. The second half of the twentieth century has been regarded by many as a phase of the triumph of democracy.

The "Free and Open Indo-Pacific Strategy" is a joint strategic vision by the United States, Australia, Japan and India. The "Quad" wants the Indo-Pacific region to be utilized in a way that will benefit everybody without any influence. The free and open maritime order in the Indo-Pacific region is to develop trade and commerce bringing stability and prosperity as well as securing peace in the region as a whole. India's engagement with the US led Quardrilateral Security Dialogue perhaps influences long-drawn India-China negotiation for disengagement in the Galwan Valley far more directly. The US trade war with China and more recently US led anti China tirade over covid-19 pandemic has surely encouraged India's boycott China campaign.

While India has had a longstanding relationship with Europe, it has largely been dominated by trade. The European Union and India have a shared interest in maintaining a rules-based order and supporting the importance role of regional institutions such as ASEAN and the Indian Ocean Rim Association. Going beyond the shared foundational interests, both Brussels and New Delhi have made efforts to expand their trade-dominated ties to include wider political, strategic, and geo-economic interests. The key areas of interest between the two governments began with infrastructure development and maritime security. In December 2018 Brussels adopted a strategy to streamline the effort to "strengthen cooperation and the partnership" with New Delhi.[16] During the Covid 19 pandemic virtual 15th India -EU Summit held on July 15. 2020 discuss on global cooperation and solidarity to protect lives, mitigate socio-economic consequences and strengthen preparedness and response capacities. They will continue working together to promote debt sustainability including in the G-20.[17] This Summit held that time when tension is rising between India and China. Lat one decade EU had given priorities to China over India. Now EU ties with New Delhi more substantively towards strengthen rules based global order.

With the continuous 'growth' and impact of 'technology driven globalization', the North-South relations are looking more stable now than previous era. 'Human Development Report-2013' also states that the precariously rooted inequalities of power, massive gaps in quality of life are now wiping out from South countries. Therefore, South is rising and there is no alternative for North to accept the rise of South that is the reason that G-20 is more relevant than G-7. Also, the globally spreading 'terrorism' is a threat in front of world that needs a 'collective war against terrorism' to abolish its roots. 'Climate change' is another threat which cannot be resolved without global concern. Therefore, this is the great responsibility for world to stand collectively against these threats in a stable global order.

International relations specialists advocate that any realistic examination of global multilateral initiatives should begin with demarcating the level of engagements, cooperation and the prospect of institutional capability.[18] It is argued, "International institutions occur when states wish to maximize sovereignty but are willing to sacrifice it in order to gain common and collective goods, as they realize that these goods are beyond their own individual capacities and that they need to pool resources."[19]

After the India is being remain as a roaring capitalist and emerging strategic partner of the United States. Indian unique development model—relying on domestic consumption and high-tech services—has brought a quarter century of record growth despite an incompetent and heavy-handed state. India's rise is not that it is new, but its path has been unique compared with the other Asian countries. Rather than adopting the classic Asian strategy exporting labour-intensive, low-priced manufactured goods to the West, India has relied on its domestic market more than exports, consumption more than investment, services more than industry, and high-tech more than low-skilled manufacturing.

The white paper of China also notes that there is a serious disequilibrium in the relative strength of countries, no fundamental change has been made order and that hegemony and power politics still exist and are developing further in the international political, economic and security spheres. Thus, the white paper argues that the powerfulness of China will constitute no threat to anyone, but will rather promote.....world peace, stability and development.[20] Although Beijing supports the principles of non-proliferation, it also maintains that peaceful use of technology should be promoted, and it continues to have serious reservations about the existing multilateral expert control regimes.[21] Similarly, the annual report of India's ministry of external affairs of entry years of 21st century notes as one of its priorities the need to strengthen further India's role as a factor for peace, stability and security and balance in Asia and in the world and to work towards strengthening peace, stability and multipolarity in the world.[22]

The triangular relationship of India-China-US is also driven by different dynamics and affects India and China differently. India worries that China will play permanent membership card in the United Nations Security Council to stop New Delhi to gets appropriate place on the world stage, whereas Beijing fears that India will play its democracy card to become more assertive in dealing with China. Similarly, on the critical issue of non proliferation, Beijing a nuclear power ambitious curbed, whereas New Delhi is keen on achieving exactly that status and is more concerned with China's reported nuclear and missile transfers to Pakistan.

The rapid aging of Chinese population attributed to its one child policy implemented over two generations will impact its domestic economic growth. On the other hand, while India is at present one tenth in size of China, it will experience accelerated growth in less than ten years with better infrastructure political reforms and financial transparency. Also, India will refocus on manufacturing both for global supply as well as for its domestic demand. Second, the global integration of India and China will be radically different. India's economy and enterprises will be globally integrated especially with other advanced countries. Even when conditions were ripe for normalizing relations from a purely bilateral point of view, India and China had to content with circumstances that affected the pace and the scope of their rapprochement. The post-cold war, Post-Pokhran, Post-11 September 2001 and Covid-19 era create a new context within which Sino-Indian relations will evolve.

Today, in a rapidly changing world order, an entirely new architecture is being formed in the global economy, politics and security. And on how relations develop between the two leading economies of Asia, not only determines the stability of the region, but also the direction of global politics for decades to come. The US-India-China pivot has been of importance in the modern history of the two Asian giants and seems to be moving towards global prominence, in political, as well as, economic terms. Currently economics is taking the lead with the Indian government hoping to fulfill its social agendas through the Make-in-India initiative complemented by the Chinese dollar reserves seeking out fresh investment ventures and American corporate machinery looking for fresh pastures for profits.

The US efforts to mentor India to soft-balance China in the Asia-Pacific gave a new dimension to the triangular relationship. While economic engagement with China has brought economic benefits for centuries in the region, China's military rise has given rise to consternation, if not outright fear, in the minds of the leaders of these countries. The United States, which has been the resident power in the region, reinvigorated its strategic engagement there. Many countries in the region are now looking towards

India not only for economic engagement, but also for strategic reassurance to soft-balance China.

The National Security strategy the report asserted that the US and India are building a strategic partnership that is underpinned by our shared interests, our shared values as the world's two largest democracies, and close connections among our people. The report further added, We value India's growing leadership on a wide array of global issues, through groups like G-20, and will seek to work with India to promote stability in South Asia and elsewhere in the world. US national security advisor James Jones, in his comments during a media briefing said: India with our growing relationship, is one of the defining partnership of the 21st century.[23]

In market economic era, the competition is normally necessary, but cooperation is the only way for two countries to go with other Asian nations. Therefore, a middle solution is that China goes for regional social and economic cooperation in Asia through collective leadership with India coordinating with other Asian partners. India's emerging and participating in the collective leadership joining hands with China and Japan in Asian regional unification process shall put impact upon the geopolitical power structure of the Asia, and cooperating with US and EU making a true multipolar world.

Samuel Huntington rightly pointed out that India, China and United States, all the three of the countries as core states of seven civilizations. The United States largest strategic rival in the Asian continent is, or soon will be, China. The United States generally frames the Chinese in the context of Northeast Asian regional matters and in the context of Japanese, Korean and Russian relations. India on the other hand, sees China has a neighbourhood rival, as the two countries often vie for influence in Southeast Asia and in the Himalayan states. People of India are in favour of India-United States strategic relationship, as India could be a counter weight to rising China in the region. Stephen Cohen rightly concluded that India will continue to see Americas power as essentially constraining, if it is not totally supportive.[24] So United States require to evolve the supportive policy toward resurgent India.[25]

Covid-19 has been a major turning point for all the countries across the globe. The fact that it started to spread from China is a key factor in shaping global politics. Since the Chinese did not warn about the serious outbreak of the virus and its consequences, many lives have been lost and is still being a victim to the virus and every country has gone through a serious economic depression that will take months from now to regain their position back in line. The geopolitical swings in the Indo-Pacific have intensified the role of regional actors along with several extra-regional actors. China being one of the leading trading partners for the ASEAN countries, the impact of the pandemic is growing more and more every day. The Quad countries are co-operating together on issues like vaccine development, financial assistance, future economy and more during this time to make their bond more promising and effective in the future.[26] The individual impact on every country would shape the future of the geopolitics in the region with China being a less reliable and less promising country for other players in the region. ASEAN and Quad will play a vital role in the post-pandemic world adapting themselves to the shifts in economies.

The present situation in Taiwan and the protests in Hong Kong with regards to independence and the influence of the US in the state have all provoked the Chinese for more assertion and rough handling of the crisis. The aggressive posture of China in the South China Sea is another huge factor that determines its relationship with other powers. The post-pandemic world is going to a lot of tilts and new dimensions in international relations, especially in the Indo-Pacific as it is emerging. India is one of the key players will have to assess every move closely as both China and the US are already competing for it in the region.

India and the US both have a common interest in the region which includes the rule of law and democratic principle, promoting global security, stability and economic prosperity through trade, investment and connectivity. Both are concerned about the visible possibility of China enhancing its influence by funding infrastructure projects in the neighbourhood of India. The Hambantota Port in Sri Lanka, The Belt and Road Initiative, China-Pakistan Economic Corridor, Chinese interference in Nepal, Bhutan and in Chabahar port that posses a great challenge to India.

All this shows how effectively India will have to strategize its influence and presence in the region as China is challenging India's historical dominance in the region. At the same time, the United States also shares a similar fear of China's growing influence militarily in the South China Sea. The main purpose of the Asia rebalancing policy is to maintain balance on the rising Chinese influence in the region. According to Rischard M. Rossow, Senior Adviser and Wadhwani Chair in US-India Policy Studies, "If India is indeed to be a central pillar of the US vision for the Indo-Pacific; it must be more deeply consulted in the development of a US strategy which reflects the interests of both strategic partners." The US and India must jointly develop a common strategy that acknowledges the Chinese challenge in the region. It is important how to reduce the conflicts & promote the world's two largest developing countries cooperation, and impact on the international political order which need the people and politicians between the countries find the new cooperative development direction under the multipolar world system.

References

1. Annual report of Indian ministry of external affairs 2007-08
2. Delpech Therese,"Nuclear weapons and the New world order" early warning from Asia? Survival 40:4 (winter 1998-99) p.62
3. O'Neill, Jim (2001): Building Better Global Economic BRICs. Goldman Sachs Global Economic Paper No. 66
4. Panda, Jagannath P, A "BRICS" Wall? The Complexity of China-India Multilateral Politics, Indian Foreign Affairs Journal, Vol. 7, No. 2, April-June 2012, p. 176.
5. Wilson Dominic and Purushothaman Roopa "Dreaming with the BRICS: The path to 2050", global economics paper no. 99, New York, Gold man sachs, 1 Oct 2003
6. Chinaview, September 27.2008
7. Garver John W., "Protracted contest: Sino-Indian rivalry in the twentieth century", University of Washington press, Seattle, 2008 p. 226-231
8. "India – China cooperation vital to save environment: report", The Hindu March 19, 2010 9. "Russia India, China agree to cooperate in energy, global issues", India Today in Beijing, February 3, 2015
10. Panda, Jagannath P "A BRICS wall? Complexity of China-India multilateral politics", Indian foreign affairs journal, Vol. ·7, No.-2 April-June 2012 p. 176
11. C. Raja Mohan, "Samudra Manthan: Sino-Indian rivalry in the Indian pacific", Washington DC: Carnegie endowment for international peace, 2012, pp. 16, 32
12. Josukutty C.A. "INDIA-U.S. Relations and Asian Rebalancing." ISBN: 978-81-7708-415-3 Published: July 2015, New Century Publications, New Delhi.
13. *https://www.state.gov/wp-content/uploads/2019/11/Free-and-Open-IndoPacific4Nov2019.pdf*

14. *https://www.iiss.org/events/shangri-la-dialogue/shangri-la-dialogue-2018*

15. *https://thegeopolitics.com/act-far-east-policy-indias-bear-hug/*

16. "EU Shapes Its Ambitious Strategy on India," press release, European Union, November 20, 2018, *https://ec.europa.eu/commission/presscorner/detail/en/IP_18_6481*

17. *https://www.mea.gov.in/bilateraldocuments.htm?dtl/32827/Joint_Statement_of_the_15th_IndiaEU_Summit_July_15_2020*

18. Galbreath David, 'International Regimes and Organizations', in Trevor C. Salmon and Mark F. Imber (eds), Issues in International Relations (2nd Edition), London: Routledge, 2008, p.122.

19. Ibid., p. 124.

20. Ministry of external affairs, government of India, Annual Report, 2000-2001 (New Delhi: government of India, 2001), pp. ii-iii

21. Ministry of Defence government of India ¯Annual Report, 2000-2001 (New Delhi: government of India, 2001), pp. 7

22. Indian ministry of Defence, ¯Annual Report, 2000-2001, p.9

23. "India among key centers of influence" in Obama security strategy, Hindustan Times, May 28, 2010, accessed on February 1, 2015

24. Stephen P Cohens, "India Emerging Power", Brooking Institute press, 2001, 155

25. Outlook India, "The United States of America and India- A Transformed relationship", Ambassador Richard Haass, 7th Jan 2003.

26. *https://www.mea.gov.in/pressreleases.htm?dtl/32691/Cooperation_among_select_countries_of_the_Indo Pacific_in_ fighting_COVID19_pandemic*

3

China's Growing Influence in Indian Ocean Region: Analysis and Implications

Lt.Gen. Nitin Kohli

> "Accelerate its (PLAN) transformation and modernisation in a sturdy way, and make extended preparations for warfare in order to make greater contributions to safeguard national security[1]"
>
> Hu Jintao, 7 December 2011

Introduction

Over the past few decades, both China and India have emerged as major regional powers, in fact even *reckonable* global powers. This has also been accompanied by their increased interactions at bilateral and multilateral levels. It is true that the two countries have often capitalized on the opportunities of geo-political convergence. But their competition and rivalry too, are increasingly evident. Events also indicate various forms of politico-diplomatic dissonance

---

Director General Signals, New Delhi

between the two, which flow from historic contentions as also the contemporary geo-political environment. In the coming years the growing power asymmetry in favour of China and stakes of both countries in the emerging global order are also likely to influence Sino-India relations.

Over time China has progressively increased its influence in South and South East Asia by leveraging diplomacy coupled with financial assistance, infrastructure development projects, investments and other economic tools, including inexpensive military hardware i.e. its 'soft power'. While existence of a common land border has largely shaped and limited Sino-Indian interactions to the terrestrial domain thus far, Chinese attention is increasingly turning to the maritime realm. In fact there has been a discernible strengthening of the PLA Navy and the PLA Air Force to win command of the sea and air as also to carry out strategic counter-strikes, as evident from study of China's Defence White Papers from 2004 onwards.

PLA's current modernization programme is focused towards vastly improving its Navy's capabilities with a view to achieve 'major power' status in a compressed time frame. It is assessed that China is likely to increase its military/naval presence in the Indian Ocean Region (IOR) in future, in close cooperation with Myanmar, Bangladesh, Sri Lanka, Pakistan, Maldives, Seychelles and numerous East African coastal states as the leapfrogging modernisation of PLA Navy progresses. The deployment of PLA Naval ships off Somali coast for anti-piracy duties is probably just the beginning of an era of Chinese presence in the Indian Ocean.

Strategic Importance of the Indian Ocean Region (IOR)

As the third-largest body of water in the world, containing vital sea lanes that help feed some of Asia's major economies, the significance of the Indian Ocean has long been known. However, the relative decline of US power in the region has created an opportunity which both China and India are keen to exploit. This confluence of events and interests is shaping the strategic developments in the region. The sea lanes in the Indian Ocean are considered among the most strategically important in the world - according to the *Journal of the Indian Ocean Region*, more than 80 percent of the world's seaborne trade in oil transits through Indian Ocean choke points, with 40 percent passing through the Strait of Hormuz, 35 percent through the Strait of Malacca and 8 percent through the Bab el-Mandab Strait[2].

The highest tonnage of global maritime trade and vital hydro-carbons transit through the Indian Ocean, with about 100,000 ships plying its waters annually. Roughly 40% of this sea-borne trade passes through the Malacca Straits. The Persian Gulf and adjoining region accounts for 50% of the world's container cargo and 33% of bulk cargo. Everyday 15.5 million barrels of oil passes through the Straits of Hormuz and 11 million barrels go through the Malacca Strait[3]. This Ocean also comprises states with disparate levels of economic and social development, governance and political maturity. Transnational terrorism and radicalism emanating from the region have risen and recent terrorist attacks in Mumbai and Jakarta are grim reminders of this reality. Threats to maritime good order – piracy, narco-terrorism, gunrunning, human smuggling and the like can suddenly erupt into a crisis, which in turn can lead to massive disruption in the global trade and energy flow, including that of China. In such a scenario, China, and also the rest of the world, appreciates the utmost need to secure these vital Sea Lanes of Communications (SLOCs).

As a result, some of the world's major powers have deployed substantial military forces in the Indian Ocean region. For example, in addition to maintaining expeditionary forces in Iraq and Afghanistan, the US 5th Fleet is headquartered in Bahrain, and uses the island of Diego Garcia as a major naval aviation base and logistics hub for its Indian Ocean operations[4]. In addition, the United States has deployed several major naval task forces there, including Combined Task Force 152, which is aimed at safeguarding the flow of oil through the Persian Gulf and Combined Task Force 150, which is tasked with countering piracy from the Gulf of Oman to Kenya[5].

China's aggressive soft power diplomacy is seen to be one of the important elements in shaping the Indian Ocean strategic environment in recent times. By providing large loans on generous repayment terms, investing in major infrastructure projects such as the building of roads, dams, ports, power plants and railways, and offering military assistance and political support in the UN Security Council through its veto powers, China has secured considerable influence among countries in the Indian Ocean region and in Straits of Malacca, Lombok, Mandeb and Sunda in South East Asia[6].

Taking the case of People's Republic of China (PRC), it cannot be denied that her strategic focus till now continues to be on the Pacific and not on the Indian Ocean region. It would however be a folly to ignore the gradually unfolding changes in the perceptions of Beijing on the IOR's strategic importance[7]; they are indeed pointers to the future. The first firm signal that maritime security interests dominate China's thinking on the IOR came through a statement (Galle, Sri Lanka, 13 December 2012) made by Vice Admiral Su Zhiqian, Commander of the East China Sea Fleet of the Chinese Navy. It laid stress on the 'freedom and safety of the navigation in the Indian Ocean' acting as a crucial factor in global economy and declared that the Chinese navy will actively maintain the peace and stability of the Indian Ocean through carrying out 'maritime security cooperation' with the navies of various countries, especially seeking to establish a maritime security 'code of conduct' between them under the 'premise of respect for each country's sovereignty and maritime interests'.

Choke Points and their Impact on Trade and Energy Transport

The marine geography of the IOR highlights the importance of major chokepoints. Securing SLOCs is vital, as they are crucial for trade, energy securityand thus the economy as a whole. Given the rapidly multiplying demand for energy, it is inevitable that countries such as Japan, India and China will remain sensitiveto the security of SLOCs and choke points of theregion. Prominent choke points of the Indian Ocean are described in brief description[8]:-

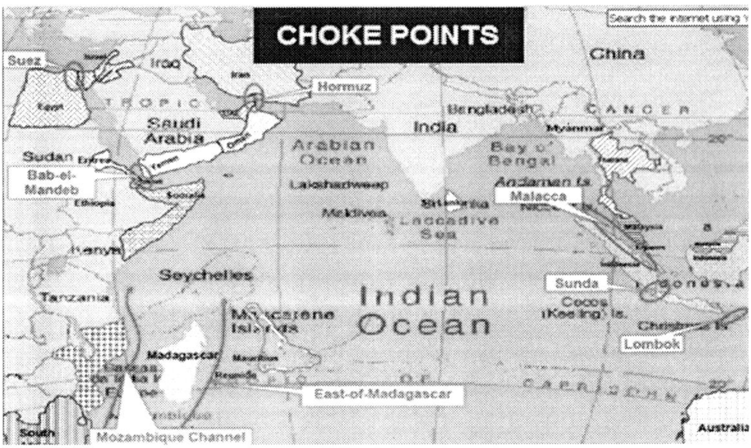

(a) **The Suez Canal**. The Suez Canal is an artificial sea-level water channel, connecting the Mediterranean Seawith the Red Sea. Inaugurated in 1869, it cuts down the shipping route dramatically. Owned and maintained by the Suez Canal Authority, it may be used "in time of war as in time of peace, by every vessel of commerce or of war, without distinction of flag[9]."

(b) **The Strait of Bab-el-Mandeb**. Bab el-Mandab acts as a strategic link between the Indian Ocean and the Mediterranean Sea, via the Red Sea and the Suez Canal.

In 2006, an estimated 3.3 million barrels (520,000 m3) of oil passed through the strait per day, out of a world total of about 43 million barrels per day (6,800,000 m3/d) moved by tankers[10].

(c) **The Strait of Hormuz**. The Strait of Hormuz is a strait between the Gulf of Oman and the Persian Gulf. It is the only sea passage from the Persian Gulf to the open ocean and is one of the world's most strategically important choke points. On the north coast is Iran, and on the south coast is the United Arab Emirates and Musandam, an exclave of Oman.

(d) **Mozambique Channel**. The Mozambique Channel is an arm of the Indian Ocean located between Madagascar and Mozambique.

(e) **Strait of Malacca**. The Strait of Malacca is a narrow stretch of water between the Peninsula andSumatra, Indonesia. It is one of the most important shipping lanes in the world. If the strait were closed, nearly half of the world's fleet would be required to sail further, with attendant implications.

(f) **Strait of Sunda**. The Sunda Strait connects the Java Sea to the Indian Ocean. It is 50 miles long and is an alternative to the Malacca Strait. Its North Eastern entrance is 15 miles wide. However, since the Northern end is relatively shallow with hazardous currents, its usage is restricted and deep-draught ships do not normally prefer the Strait.

(g) **Strait of Lombok**. The Lombok Strait connects the Java Sea to the Indian Ocean, and runs between the Indonesian islands of Lombok and Bali. Though longer than the Strait of Malacca, it is wider and deeper and not draught-limited. It is thus favoured by large vessel over 100,000 DWT. Most ships transiting the Lombok Strait also pass through the Makassar Strait which is more suited for submarines and large ships[11].

Indian SLOCs originate and also terminate in this region and therefore re-routing of ships through the waters that flow from the choke points like the Gulf of Aden and the Malacca Strait is not an option available to India. In comparative terms although, for China, re-routing via the Lombok and Sunda Straits is an alternative, with attendant effects on delivery factor in terms of time and the requirement todivert naval assets to cover these maritime areas.

From India's perspective it becomes imperative to contain Chinese influence in the IOR and ensure protection of both military and economic interests. Picking a leaf from larger maritime powers in the past, over the last two decades India has tackled its interests in the Indian Ocean littorals, straddling those in Asia (Mauritius, Maldives, Seychelles and Madagascar) as also those in East Africa (Mozambique, Tanzania and South Africa) by adroit application of foreign policy, generous hand out of economic sops, and international defence cooperation. Thus by deft diplomacy and presentation of economic packages, India too is gaining influence. Diplomacy includes the complete gambit of naval vessel transfers, provision of staff and training, hydrographic support and access to refit facilities. These steps have made a significant impact on the recipient states.

Geographical Significance of Andaman & Nicobar Islands

Geography bestows upon India certain unique advantages in this great game as it were and should be leveraged. India will always retain a sizeable advantage over any incoming Chinese fleet in the Indian Ocean by virtue of its central position as an interior line power in the heart of the Indian Ocean, which enables radiation of maritime and airpower in an arc extending from the Malacca Straits in the East to the Arabian Sea in the West. Any Chinese fleet would therefore have to face a formidable gauntlet of combined Indian naval and shore-based airpower in the Indian Ocean.

Add to the above, the strategic location of the Andaman & Nicobar Islands. The Andaman and Nicobar Command, which came into being in 2001, is of vital strategic significance. Separated from the mainland India by approximately 1200 Km of sea, the island chain, constitutes the nation's Eastern maritime defence perimeter. At a strategic level the A&N islands could effectively be viewed as a static aircraft carrier deployed on the Eastern Seaboard.

It has also been described by certain Chinese analysts as a 'metal chain' which could lock China out of the Indian Ocean. It goes without saying that the island command will play a first line role in the event of a Sino-Indian naval clash in the Indian Ocean. Measures have been taken to strengthen India's force presence on the islands, most notably by enlarging airstrips for use by Sukhois[12], or by announcing the stationing of India's first full-bodied joint amphibious force and the ramping up of its existing 3000 strong Mountain Brigade to a division level force of 15000 troops[13].

Modernisation of PLA Navy

China looks at the IOR from two perspectives. The first is centered on the security of its SLOCs on which its growing economy is heavily dependent. The second stems from the need of any emerging power to be relevant and present in all active spots, so as to be able to favourably influence events in its national interest. For both of these China (PLA) needs a capable modern Navy.

Historically, PLA Navy has not been a strong contemporary force. Yet, driven by steady economic growth and comprehensive national power, China has actively begun to increase its naval capabilities in the last decade, by pursuingnew domestic projects and continuing notable acquisitions from Russia. The PLA Navy has been stressing upon improving its capabilities for integrated offshore operations, strategic deterrence and strategic counter attacks[14], and is gradually developing its capability for conducting international cooperation in distant waters and countering non-traditional security threats.

As a corollary, the PRC's naval objectives have undergone a shift – from that of conducting coastal defence activities to offshore defence and ultimately to far sea defence[15]. A case in point is the stress noticed in China's latest Defence White Paper (2013) on "protecting national maritime rights and interests" and "armed forces providing reliable support for China's interests overseas[16]". It is clear that the PRC intends to expand the capabilities of its Navy, especially to operate abroad; this indeed marks a new stage in China's development which has come into being due to the increasing needs being felt by a rising China to secure its growing global interests[17].

Three primary objectives are perceived to be behind the PLA Navy's modernization programme. The first can be attributed to the conflict potential within the Taiwan Strait. The second related issue may be the perception of an increased threat posed by the significant US naval presence in the Pacific Ocean. The third factor is the desirability to develop a 'blue water' fleet and secure its SLOCs, particularly those passing though the Indian Ocean and the South China Sea. It is the third factor which has witnessed the recent increase in the frequency of the PLA Navy's forays into the Indian Ocean.

As the PLA Navy aims at enhancing its strategic reach and to push its maritime defence perimeter seaward, it requires modern naval hardware, additional infrastructure tosupport the growing force size, transformed operational doctrines, tactics and procedures and a matching manpower profile[18]. All the above efforts are well supported by her growing economy and the consequent increase in the Chinese defence budget. Barring 2010, when the budget grew by

7.5%, there has been a double digit growth for more than a decade. With the PLA Navy being accorded top priority in the modernisation drive, it is estimated that about 24% of this outlay is allocated to the PLA Navy[19].

Over the last decade, the Navy has been decommissioning older ships and inducting modern units. The PLA Navy is pursuing a two-pronged programme, viz acquisition of advanced technology based strategic assets indigenous development and production of platforms and weapon systems. The main acquisitions include four Sovremenny class guided missile destroyers with advancedanti-submarine warfare Kamov 28 helicopters and eight kilo 636 class diesel driven submarines armed with '3M-54E' cruise missiles. The indigenous production includes the building and commissioning of the Shang class nuclear powered attack submarines, Jin class nuclear powered ballistic missile carrying submarines,Luyang I and II class multi-role destroyers, Jiangkai I and II class guided missile frigates and the Yuzhao class large amphibious ship. Amphibious warfare capabilities are also being augmented by way of significant equipment upgrades, including induction of new amphibious tanks, Armoured Personnel Carriers (APCs) and the aircushion landing craft probably 'Zubr' class air cushion landing crafts (LCAC)from Russia. The PLA Navy is also renovating its Varyag aircraft carrier indigenously and reportedly has plans to construct up to two more carriers by 2020[20].

The ship construction infrastructure is also being up-scaled with a view to undertake indigenous construction of China's first aircraft carrier in near future. A large shipyard complex at Changxing Island off Shanghai, which has a dry dock capable of undertaking construction of an aircraft carrier of up to 70000 tons displacement, has reportedly been constructed. The largest dock is 580 m long and 120 m wide and an aircraft carrier's model has been displayed in one of the dry docks in the scaled mock-up of the Changxing Ship-building Base[21]. A full scale land based model of the Varyag carrier has also been constructed at Wuhan in the central Chinese province of Hubei for possibly training Chinese pilots for carrier based landing and take-off.

Although not much information is available about the PLA Navy's capacity building in the IOR, her overall capability is very much in public view, particularly in South and East China Sea maritime areas. China has constructed an underground nuclear submarine berthing facility at the South Sea Fleet base on Hainan Island and the PLA Navy's Jin class SSBNs were recently reported as having been based there. This base is in addition to the one previously constructed at Jianggezhuang in the North Sea Fleet's area of responsibility. The base is likely to have extensive underground facilities which could include a canal to house at least one submarine, equipment handling and storage space as well as accommodation for personnel. The facilities at the PLA Navy's Woody Island base in the Paracel group of islands, about 180 nautical miles (NM) South East of Hainan Island are also being upgraded to enable its ships and the PLA Navy Air Force to extend its sea and aerial coverage area further seawards into the South China Sea. A runway of about 8000 feet and the logistical infrastructure including ship berthing facilities exist there[22].

The doctrine, tactics and procedures of the PLA Navy all emanate from a combined PLA's military strategy of "Active Defence". The "offshore defence" strategy[23] is the naval component of the "active defence" strategic guidelines which directs the PLA Navy to "defend the country's maritime rights, interests and security, safeguard its economic development and serve its peaceful diplomacy[24]' by engaging in maritime operations in it's offshore area. It also seeks to strengthen its capability to effectively control the major sea routes linking China's waters, when necessary, and to operate in the seas adjacent to China's maritime territory. China is also likely to increase its military/naval presence in the Indian Ocean Region (IOR) in future, in close cooperation with littoral states.

The personnel intake, training and remuneration patterns of the PLA Navy have also undergone a sea change in the last decade so as to supplement the ongoing modernisation drive. The PLA Navy, as part of its "talent training project"[25], launched in 2003, has signed agreements with 16 civilian higher learning institutions since 1999 for raising the technical skill. The PLA Navy has revised the recruitment regulations to enlist college students for the first time. Salaries of the PLA personnel were doubled in 2006 after remaining stagnant for about 20 years. These were further revised in March 2009. With this increase, the military personnel would get about 20% higher salaries than the salaries for civil servants placed in similar positions. All these new initiatives are expected to improve the military structure in terms of the skill set required.

Aero-Space Capabilities

China is investing heavily into developing her aero-space capabilities. By 2020 China can reasonably be expected to have the following aero-space capability[26]:

(a) More than 1,000 fourth generation multirole tactical aircraft and a start on deploying two fifth generation tactical aircraft and a fully panoply of modern weapons, with increasingly long range, to go with them.

(b) A reasonable airlift capability.

(c) A significant Unmanned Aerial System (UAS) capability.

(d) A modern IADS Integrated Air Defence System (IADS) covering the most important regions of China and extending to cover the Taiwan Strait and possibly much of Taiwan.

(e) A large force of long-range precision-guided ballistic and cruise missiles, including a substantial force of antiballistic missiles and precision-guided ballistic missiles able to cover the seas around China and threaten Naval bases as far as 5000 Km away.

(f) A significant (possibly major) anti-satellite capability and potentially a significant capacity for space warfare.

(g) A rudimentary (but emerging) force of aircraft carriers carrying at least fourth generation aircraft. China may also have a significant amphibious capability.

(h) A manned space capability that will approach, if not surpass, the capabilities of the mature American Apollo system and quite possibly both manned and unmanned shuttles.

(i) The research, development, and industrial capability necessary to support all this.

If integrated with modern C4ISR systems, applied with an effective joint strategy, and used effectively, China could pose a major threat to surface ships operating within the First Island Chain (in the Yellow Sea, Taiwan Strait, East China Sea, and at least much of the South China Sea), and pose at least some threat to bases as far away as Guam.

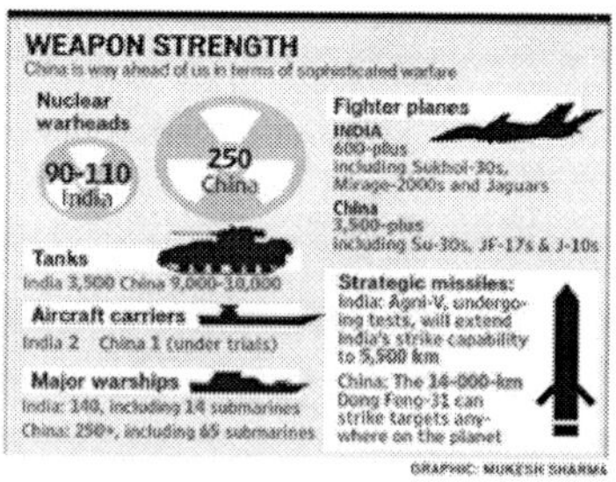

A comparison of Indian and Chinese military strengths, as above shows the visible asymmetry in favour of China[27].

The Chinese have undertaken a comprehensive development program of aero-space. They are clearly pursuing methodical and rapid modernization of their air, air defence, missile, and space capabilities. Further, they are updating their C4ISR capabilities to build a system capable of joint net-centric operations and able to provide targeting for Chinese standoff weapons, including some degree of real-time targeting for their ASBMs.

Although only partly completed, in the aggregate all of these provide the Chinese with the potential for revolutions both in aero-space technology and in military capabilities. Further, over time their designs increasingly have come from domestic Chinese sources. In any case, the number of new and modified aircraft and missile designs and prototypes being developed simultaneously is impressive and indicates a large and competent design capability.

String of Pearls - Power Projection & Distrust

Christopher J. Pehrson, US Army War College,author of the book "String of Pearls: Meeting the challenge of China's rising power across the Asian littoral", says the 'String of Pearls' describes the manifestation of China's rising geopolitical influence through efforts to increase access to ports and airfields, develop special diplomatic relationships[28] and modernize military forces that extend from the South China Sea through the Strait of Malacca, across the Indian Ocean, and on to the Arabian Gulf.[29] The String of Pearls is therefore a euphemism

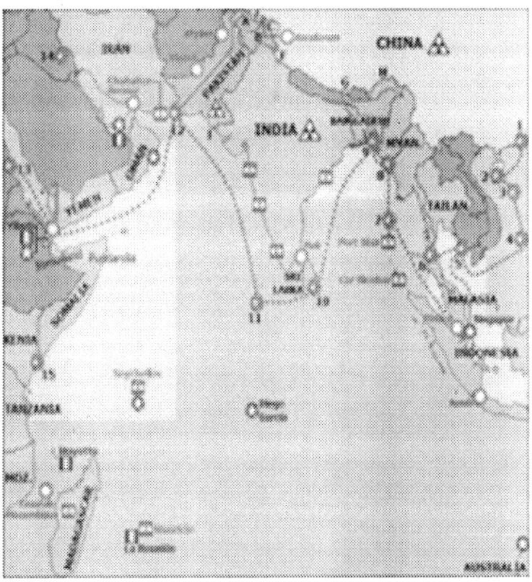

for strategic encirclement through a network of Chinese facilities (military and commercial) and relationships along its sea lanes of communication and will provide China with forward presence and military bases along the SLOCs from China to the Persian Gulf in the Middle East. At one level of abstraction this can be viewed as pearls tied to a string, where each pearl represents a port in a country to which China has access and the string represents the Sea Lanes of Communication (SLOCs). A pearl normally comes with facilities like airstrips and naval bases.

The First Pearl is generally considered to be the Hainan Island in South China, where a massive underground submarine and warship base has been built, because of its strategic location in the South China Sea[30]. The Second Pearl is the port of Hambantota in Sri Lanka. Inspite of the objection from India, phase I of the project is already complete and balance phases are underway. China is underwriting a US$1.2 billion package for the facility. China's investment in this area will increase significantly as it apparently has interest in oil drilling in North East Sri Lanka. Hambantota port will also include aviation fuel storage facility, LNG refinery and a bunkering facility[31] to refuel ships. The Third Pearl is located at the Chittagong port in Bangladesh. The Fourth is the Woody Island located 300 miles East of the Paracel Archipelago. An airstrip has been upgraded for this purpose[32]. The Port of Sittwe in Myanmar, Marao Atoll in the Maldives and Gwadar Port in Pakistan complete the picture. The Gwadar port comes with a naval base and it is chosen because of its strategic value in the 240 Km distance from the Straits of Hormuz. The Karakoram Highway, which connects China's Xinjiang region with Pakistan's North, can also be seen as one of China's pearls[33]. The highway, called the ninth wonder of the world by some because of its altitude, was completed in 1986 after 20 years of construction[34].

For both Pakistan and China, the Gwadar port offers a number of port key benefits. It is seen as having the potential of hedging against a potential Indian blockade of the port of Karachi, which currently handles 90% of Pakistani seaborne trade. For the Chinese central government, which has funded the majority of the $1.2 billion construction, Gwadar represents an important strategic foothold situated only 240 miles from the Strait of Hormuz[35]. Chinese government officials have specifically identified the growing militarization of Central Asia, as a chief motivation in the construction of the Gwadar project[36]. In 2013, the state-owned China Overseas Port Holding Company was officially granted control of the port's operation, further consolidating Chinese influence over the Gwadar project[37].

The Chinese government has financed a container shipping facility in Chittagong, Bangladesh, which is widely identified as[38] a pearl. However, despite reports of Chittagong's potential for the Chinese, the Government of Bangladesh maintains otherwise. Furthermore, given Bangladesh's close ties with India, albeit dependent on the political party in power, military significance of Chittagong for the Chinese may well be over estimated.

Strategists have also identified the Marao Atoll, in the Maldives, as a potential Chinese military base of operations[39]. However, to date there is no evidence to suggest that Chinese military presence of any kind in the Maldives. Indeed, it is argued that Marao Atoll cannot possibly support the type of complex infrastructure required for submarine operations. Given the nature of diplomatic and military cooperation between India and the Maldives, exploitation of Maldives Archipelago by the Chinese is a moot issue.

Well, it is a fact that seaports that can accommodate container ships and the like can also accommodate fighting ships for routine functions such as refueling and re-provisioning. They can be further improved to serve as full-up naval stations. In short, Beijing is creating options for[40] itself. Whether it chooses to exercise that option will depend on how swiftly and fully Chinese naval power matures, how successfully Beijing manages events closer to home, and how menacing the South Asian strategic environment appears[41]. It may be realized that, great powers generate options to hedge against the unknown.

But converting a commercial port into a fully operational military base is a major effort and not likely to escape the attention of the vigilant. Even if China were to convince / coerce the host nation to permit such a project to develop say Gwadar or Colombo into naval base it would in all likelihood be at the cost of antagonizing India, the regional power. Further, such negotiations and actions cannot be carried out covertly, i.e. they are conspicuous. This will give regional and extra-regional powers time to mull over their response. The hallmarks of a naval base as per Mahanian logic are position, resources and strength. While most identified pearls are strategically located, they also lie within the range of the Indian Air Force, as also the U.S. and Indian naval fleets.

Many analysts have suggested that Chinese Indian Ocean bases are purely commercial because they would be nearly indefensiblein wartime. They opine that a large component of China's efforts to establish ports and bases in the Indian Ocean is the result of a need to formalize logistics support agreements for Chinese naval forces conducting anti-piracy efforts off of the Horn of Africa. By Mahanian logic, seafaring people should do what China is doing, and what marine colonizing states once did. It will seek commercial, political, and military access to regions that are home to important export and import markets. What's portrayed as trade today could be set the stage for aggression or, naval power projection tomorrow.

A related development is a Chinese proposal to construct a canal across the Kra Isthmus, which would allow ships to bypass the Strait of Malacca altogether[42]. China has also broached concerns of a Chinese-controlled corridor linking Chinese ports and facilities elsewhere in the South China Sea to the Indian Ocean.

The emergence of the String of Pearls is indicative of China's growing geopolitical influence through concerted efforts to obtain access to ports and airfields, expand and modernize military forces, and foster stronger diplomatic relationships with trading partners[43]. The Chinese Government insists that China's burgeoning naval strategy is entirely peaceful in nature and designed solely for the protection of regional trade interests. That having been said, it may also be appropriate to note that China's neighbors do not seem to view this development in the same light.

China has deep anxieties about the geographical location of India that allows it to dominate the Indian Ocean. It has therefore created options for deploying its armed forces in the IOR. In turn, the establishment of a Chinese naval base in the region would have uncomfortable security implications for India. The sustained presence of PLA Navy ships in the Indian Ocean, particularly in the Arabian Sea, will restrict the availability of maritime space for the Indian Navy and limit its area of influence. This may also boost the morale of Pakistan, at a psychological level. The Indian Navy will have to factor in the presence of Chinese naval ships in the Indian backyard while planning operations, missions and exercises[44].

Analysis and Implications

China's Perspective

While there is neither any indication at present to suggest that China will set up a base in Maldives or Seychelles, nor whether Maldives or Seychelles would willingly accede toany such Chinese request, the Indian strategic and security establishment must take due cognizance of this probability turning into reality and prepare strategies to preserve the Indian national interest in the Indian Ocean and its littorals[45].

As the fastest growing Asian country, China has specifically focused on economic development in the last three decades as the bedrock of its intrinsic national strength. This growth model is naturally energy intensive. China's oil demand has been growing at more than 5% over the last decade. In its December report, the IEA estimated Chinese oil demand at 10.19 million bpd in 2013, up 370,000 bpd from 2012[46]. The agency has forecast similar, modest growth for this year at 3.7 percent to 10.57 million bpd[47]. Though its domestic production in 2009 was 189.4 million tones,[48] its dependence on imported crude oil had risen from 8% in 1994 to 48% in 2007,[49] and stands at about half of its total demand in 2009. The uninterrupted, safe and guaranteed supply of oil and gas has therefore become a serious issue for the Chinese leadership. President Hu Jintao, during a Central Party economic work committee meeting in 2003, reportedly raised Chinese energy security concerns by stating that more than 80% of Chinese imported oil has to pass through the Malacca Strait, and that China must actively adopt measures to ensure the security of its energy imports. This concern popularly came to be known as the "Malacca Strait Dilemma".[50]

The safe transportation of energy from their sources in the Persian Gulf and West Africa is therefore of the biggest concern to China. Though the incidents of piracy, robbery and maritime terrorism in South East Asian waters have been controlled to a large extent by the anti-piracy measures initiated by the littoral countries, the prospect of a rise in such incidents is always lurking. Sub-national or non-state entities like the Al Qaeda, in collaboration with resident organisations like the Jemmah Islamiyah and Abu Sayaf, may attempt to sink a ship in a narrow strait or use a Liquefied Petroleum Gas (LPG)/crude carrier as a huge bomb in a port or a busy waterway to disrupt the smooth flow of maritime trade and oil. This perception has possibly obligated China to strengthen the capacity of the PLA Navy to operate effectively at long distances from its coastline and be in a position to safeguard China's trade and energy lifelines. Chen Mingyi, member the National Committee of the Chinese People's Political Consultative Conference, exhorted the PLA Navy to "move to oceans and shoulder the tasks of safeguarding territory, development of national economy and overseas interests[51]". The Chinese White Paper 2008 also mentioned the need to conduct international cooperation in distant waters and counter non-traditional security threats just prior to the deployment of its first ever anti-piracy mission in the Gulf of Aden.

The first ever 'Out of Area' operational mission of PLA Navy commenced when an anti-piracy task force, consisting of two destroyers and a supply ship, arrived in Gulf of Aden on 6 January, 2009. Since then, the PLA Navy has deployed eight successive task forces consisting of two of its most modern destroyers/frigates, a one off LPD and a replenishment ship. The eighth task force which arrived on task in March 2011 comprises missile frigates Ma'anshan and Wenzhou and supply ship Qiandaohu[52]. China has reportedly agreed to collaborate with the CMF (Combined Maritime Force – a multi-national counter-piracy naval partnership) in the Internationally Recommended Transit corridor (IRTC) in the Gulf of Aden. The PLA Navy ships have, however, been operating about 15 to 20 NM North of the IRTC and escorting merchant ships in addition to the regular escorting service being provided in that corridor.

The Chinese Navy's field activities now include its participation in the joint anti-piracy patrols off the coast of Somalia in 2011 and its ship to ship replenishment exercise in Eastern Indian Ocean in December 2013 as well as the 'counter-piracy, search, rescue and damage control drill', carried out in January 2014 by a three-ship Chinese navy squadron[53]. In the last mentioned, the largest amphibious Chinese landing ship –Changbaishan – along with two destroyers took part. The choice of Lombok Strait near Indonesia, as drill location has been significant as by doing so, Beijing seems to have opened up a new route from the South China Sea to the Indian Ocean, other than the usual one used for drills through the Malacca Strait[54]. Chinese official view on the drill is to observe it as a part of 'annually held naval combat exercises in the South China Sea, the West Pacific Ocean and the East Indian Ocean to test the combat ability of naval ships[55]'.

Regional and Extra Regional Players

Three broad categories of countries are involved in the struggle for dominance in the Indian Ocean[56]. These are as follows:-

(a) The Big Players: These countries seek preponderance or influence across the entirety of the Indian Ocean. Possibly the U.S. India and China, have the resources and the will to compete at this level.

(b) Regional players: These countries seek influence mainly in the part of the Indian Ocean that is most relevant to their interests. They include South Korea, Japan, Australia, Indonesia, Malaysia, Pakistan, Iran, Israel, Russia, South Africa and the United Kingdom.

(c) Passive players: These countries are not in a position to exert influence. Instead, they will be courted by the larger powers as part of the latter's strategic reach. These states include Bangladesh, Djibouti, Madagascar, Maldives, Mauritius, Mozambique, Myanmar, Oman, the Seychelles, Somalia, Sri Lanka, and Yemen. Remote islands and overseas territories in the Indian Ocean could also become important[57].

Likely Impact on Regional Stability

The prophetic words expounding on the importance of Indian Ocean security towards the stability of India, as expressed by Panikkar the noted Indian maritime historian remain relevant till date. He stated that, "to the other countries, the Indian Ocean is only one of the important oceanic areas; to India, it is a vital sea. Her lifelines are concentrated in that area, her freedom is dependent on the freedom of that coastal surface. No industrial development, no commercial growth, no stable political structure is possible for her unless her shores are protected"[58].

The same concerns can very well be extrapolated to the stability of the whole region in light of the broad spectrum of security challenges currently existing therein. The naval forces of more than 45 countries, including many extra-regional powers, are present in the Gulf of Aden for anti-piracy operations. The US Navy is here to stay in the Indian Ocean, and this fact has been officially reiterated in unequivocal terms by stating that "credible combat power will be continuously postured in the Western Pacific and the Arabian Gulf/Indian Ocean to protect [American] vital interests and deter potential adversaries and peer competitors".

This has been further amplified by stating that "for the foreseeable future, [the US Navy will maintain continuous presence of one each Carrier Strike Group and Amphibious Readiness Group in the Arabian Gulf/Indian Ocean". Chinese academic discourse indicates that China's preoccupation with the possibility that its energy security in the Indian Ocean could become a hostage to India's maritime strategy is increasingly becoming source of anxiety to its strategic elite. Hence, even if the problem of piracy in the Arabian Sea was to be resolved, it is considered that the PLA Navy would not return to China, especially after investing so much effort, resources and international relations capital, and having gained strong sea legs, vital lessons in inter-operability and above all, a say in global maritime matters.

The continued presence of these two extra-regional navies in the Indian Ocean with the similar stated motives of "SLOC security" and "freedom of the seas" but diametrically opposite ways of thinking, does portend for instability. The rising capability of the Indian Navy also adds a third dimension into the power matrix. Robert Kaplan in fact identifies the "Indian Ocean [as the place] where the global struggles will play out in the 21st century". One Chinese author also suggests that the Indian Ocean is perceived as a guarded sphere of influence by India and offers an important arena for Beijing and New Delhi to display their strategic muscle.

One of the scenarios painted by two Indian strategists predicts that China will manage to find a military base on the East African coast and position an air expeditionary wing for providing air cover for the PLA Navy ships deployed in the region. In such a scenario, India will find herself isolated with regard to its strategic interests in the IOR[59].

Many other countries of Asia will perforce have to look for options in order to find a power balance *vis-à-vis* the proactive Chinese presence in the region. India will also have to look for alternatives to reverse this 'isolation' predicament. These dynamic sand counter-responses may impact on the regional stability.

Measures That India Should Adopt To Counter China

India's Way Forward

Considering Chinese ambitions, India has to make a sagacious move to retain the traditional influence in Indian Ocean island states. The foremost task for Indian policy makers is to augment the economic and trade cooperation with these island states. China's trade with majority of these nations has increased manifold in recent years with only modest escalation in the same time frame by India[60]. India also has to necessarily shed the impression that all decision making and follow-up action is hopelessly mired in bureaucracy.

There is requirement to enhance and coordinate economic and defiance cooperation among the IOR littorals through an active regional forum/ sub regional groupings or by rejuvenating the Indian Ocean Rim-Association for Regional Cooperation (IOR-ARC)[61].

Strong bonds with the neglected East African countries are critically important. It is also imperative for India to develop an 'East Africa policy' if it has to have an enduring presence in island states of the Western Indian Ocean.

Indo-US maritime cooperation in the Indian Ocean needs concerted attention. The two key players of the Indian Ocean, India and the U.S. can collaborate to tackle piracy and terrorism in this region, as well as to limit scope for China's aspirations. Maritime cooperation with Japan and Australia too would help.

Reliable maritime access in the Indian Ocean requires India to have true blue water naval capability, without which, the Indian Navy will be constrained to coastal waters. To sustain a 'global' economy a blue water navy capable of dominating the Indian Ocean is vital.

India needs to aggressively pursue a focused diplomatic campaign to counter Chinese influence in the IOR. Certain facets in this regards are as follows:-

(a) **Cashing on Anti-China Sentiments.** China is seen as the 'big brother' in the region, whereas India is viewed more benignly. The anti-China sentiment must be built upon and India can act as a conduit / channelise anti- Chinese sentiments. It will be a befitting response to the perceived Chinese strategic encirclement of India (*'String of Pearls'*).

(b) **Counter Diplomacy**. To counter Chinese inroads into Pakistan, India needs to cultivate relationships with nations that have strong anti-China views. Historically, China has not enjoyed good relations with Japan, Vietnam and South Korea. India could exploit its strengths to build closer ties with these countries, which in turn would also benefit India.

(c) **Indo-US Ties**. Given its naval strength, only the U.S. has the capacity to contain or even confront China in the Indian Ocean and South China Sea, should there be an occasion. Therefore, India needs to leverage its unique geographical position and economic status to forge a nuanced relationship with the U.S.

(d) **India's relation with ASEAN**. Indian interests in South East Asia are critical for its need for resources and energy security. India needs to keep closer ties with ASEAN countries to counter balance Chinese advances. South East Asia starts from India's North East. Its development would incrementally help India in improving its ties with South East Asia. The Look East Policy (LEP) which was articulated in the early 1990s needs to be pursued even more vigorously now.

(e) **Andaman & Nicobar Islands**. Keeping its strategic importance in view, India should plan on development of A & N Islands into a container trans-shipment port as the distance to International Shipping Lines is least compared to any other port in India. This will bring international focus and stakes into the area and enhance its strategic importance.

(f) **India's Unique Geography.** Peninsular India uniquely dominates the IOR and hence the SLOCs. This strategic advantage should be exploited for domination of IOR.

India needs to build up adequate military capabilities

to deter the threat from China. India's growing military muscle in region in terms of creating infrastructure and capabilities, joint exercises and training is a step towards creating a balance. Following points may be considered:-

(a) **Domination of Choke Points**. India should dominate choke points viz Malacca, Sunda, Lombok etc. It should develop surveillance and intelligence capabilities and position nuclear submarines suitably to be able to react in a shorter time frame.

(b) **Capability Building.** Greater focus and commitment is needed for development of infrastructure in the border areas and acquisition of various war fighting equipments. In this regard bureaucratic hurdles should be removed, capital acquisition process be simplified and there should be prompt decision making in addition to suitable increase in the capital defence budget.

(c) **Defence Cooperation**. We need to collaborate with foreign nations in terms of maritime reconnaissance and conduct of joint exercises in the IOR to send visible signals to the environment regarding our capabilities and intentions.

(d) **Sea Power**. Focused approach for infrastructure development in terms of building/acquisition of aircraft carriers, maritime reconnaissance capabilities and space based surveillance and communication, is required to be able to monitor and deter China from any misadventure.

(e) **C4ISR Capabilities**. We need C4ISR capabilities at the national level to have more coordinated and synergetic response to any adverse situation.

(f) **Enhancing Cyber Warfare Capabilities**. Our Cyber Warfare capability needs to be enhanced to protect our networks and systems. We also need to have Cyber Warriors operating from various parts of the world to continuously monitor intentions and capabilities of our adversaries and exploit these at the suitable time.

(g) **Coast Guard for Coastal Security**. We need to enhance the capabilities of the Coast Guard for the coastal security so that Navy can be suitably equipped and trained for the blue water mandate.

(h) **Guard against Chinese Capabilities.** The Chinese follow SunTzu's philosophy; hence we need to monitor their capabilities and not be guided by their intentions, which can change any time. We need to train and collaborate accordingly.

(j) **Monitoring platforms.** We need to have listening stations on A&N islands and also ship based ocean going platforms for obtaining signal intelligence of activities in the IOR.

India is at least 10-20 years behind China on infrastructural development. India needs to improve its decision-making processes and speed up its execution of projects to bring its infrastructure on par with that of China. This assumes importance in the North Eastern States of India where connectivity with India and also with South East Asia is vital to the integration and economic growth of the region.

Conclusion

History is littered with conflicts, explained as the inevitable clash between nations amid a change in the balance of power. In fact, it is rare that conflict does not occur as a result of power shifts. If forecasts are correct, China is soon to enter another revolutionary phase of her development, which will affect international relations.

At the heart of this transformation is the plan to urbanise some 400 million Chinese people by 2030[62]. The demand upon resources to support the infrastructure required to host the number of people in cities will dwarf current demands. It is estimated that energy consumption alone in a city is three and a half times that of rural habitation. This will place significant stress upon China's scarce resources, the global environment and make the security of energy from the Middle East and Africa of the utmost sovereign importance. It also helps to explain the voracious nature with which Chinese global energy and resource acquisition is being pursued and protected, as far as maritime security in the Indian Ocean is concerned.

The challenge for India is to create the necessary balance of power in its geo-strategic environment in order to concentrate on economic, technological and military matters indispensable to its emergence as a true great power.

Though China has many competitive edges, India too has significant edges especially in terms of her geographical location, world image and potential for strategic partnerships as well as demographic dividend that can be made use of to overcome the Chinese challenge. Conversely, China's disadvantage needs to be leveraged by India along with like-minded countries.

References

1. Hu Jintao Tells China Navy: Prepare for Warfare', BBC News China, *www.bbc.co.uk/news/world-asia-china-16063607? print=true (7 December 2011).*
2. Sergei DeSilva-Ranasinghe, Why the Indian Ocean Matters, The Diplomat, 02 Mar 2011
3. Sergei DeSilva- Ranasinghe, Understanding Asia-Pacific sea power, The Diplomat, 02 Mar 2011 for The Diplomat
4. Sergei DeSilva-Ranasinghe, Why the Indian Ocean Matters, The Diplomat, 02 Mar 2011
5. Sergei DeSilva-Ranasinghe, Understanding Asia-Pacific sea power, The Diplomat, 02 Mar 2011for The Diplomat for The Diplomat
6. Sergei DeSilva-Ranasinghe, Why the Indian Ocean Matters, The Diplomat, 02 Mar 2011

7. D.S. Rajan, The Unfolding China's Indian Ocean Strategy, Paper No. 5646, South Asia Analysis Group, 12 Feb 2014

8. Matt Rosenberg, "Chokepoints", *http://geography.about.com/library/weekly/aa052597.htm*

9. Article 1 of the Constantinople Convention of the Suez Canal.

10. *World Oil Transit Chokepoints,* Energy Information Administration, US Department of Energy.

11. Gus Lubin, "A Brief Tour Of The 7 Oil Chokepoints That Are Crucial To The World Economy", Business Insider, 05 Feb 2011.

12. Iskander Rahman, China's String of Pearls and India's Enduring Tactical Advantage, 08 June 2010.

13. Iskander Rehman, "China's String of Pearls and India's Enduring Tactical Advantage", IDSA Comment, 08 Jun 2010. *http://www.idsa.in/node/5468/368*

14. China White Paper on National Defense 2008, http:*//www.informationdissemination.net/2009/01/china-white-paper-on-national-defense.html* accessed on 21 Feb 2014

15. D. S. Rajan, The Unfolding China's Indian Ocean Strategy, Paper No. 5646, South Asia Analysis Group, 12 Feb 2014

16. D.S. Rajan ibid

17. D.S. Rajan ibid

18. Kamlesh Kumar Agnihotri, "Modernisation of the Chinese Navy, its Strategic Expansion into the Indian Ocean Region and Likely Impact on the Regional Stability", Journal of the National Maritime Foundation of India, Volume 7, Issue 1, 2011

19. Kamlesh Kumar Agnihotri ibid

20. R O Rourke, "China Naval Modernisation", Congress Research Services, US, 30 Sep 2013

21. R O Rourke, ibid
22. Andrew S Erickson, "China's Modernisation of Naval and Air Power Capabilities", Strategic Asia 2012-2013, Oct 12
23. See "Chinese Navy to Stick to Defensive Strategy" Xinhua, April 23, 2009, *http://news.xinhuanet.com/english/2009-04/23/content_11239423.htm*
24. *http://news.xinhuanet.com/english/2009-04/23/content_ 11239423.htm* ibid
25. See "Chinese DM holds briefings on Talent-training for Foreign Defence Attaches," People's Daily online, May 1, 2007. *http://english.people.com.cn/200505/01/eng20070501_371136.html*
26. Lt Col Thomas R McCabe, USAFA (Retd), "China's Air and Space Revolution, Michel Paper 10, Michel Institute Press", Apr 2013
27. Rahul Singh, "India far behind China's combat power", Hindustan Times, New Delhi, 15 Dec 2013.
28. M. Shahidul Islam, "China-Bangladesh Relations: Contemporary Convergence", The Daily Star, 25 Jan 2012
29. Patrick Mendis," The Sri Lankan Silk Road", Harvard International Review, 30 November 2012
30. Paal, Douglas H, "'Beware the South China Sea", The Diplomat, 15 July 2011.
31. Sam Chee Kong, China's String of Pearls Strategy: Why is the U.S. afraid and how does it affect us?, Malaysia Chronicle, 22 December 2013
32. Sam Chee Kong, ibid
33. Raashi Bhatia, "India encircled by China's string of pearls?", India Insight, 28 July 2009
34. Raashi Bhatia, ibid
35. Wikipedia, *http://en.wikipedia.org/wiki/String_of_Pearls_(China), accessed on 22 Feb 14*

36. Pehrson, Christopher J, "String of Pearls: Meeting the Challenge of China's Rising Power Across the Asian Littoral.", Carlisle Papers in Security Strategy, July 2006
37. Wikipedia, *http://en.wikipedia.org/wiki/String_of_Pearls_(China),* accessed on 22 Feb 14
38. Wikipedia, ibid
39. Wikipedia, ibid
40. James R. Holmes, "Don't Worry About China's String of Pearls....Yet", The Diplomat, 09 July 13
41. James R. Holmes, ibid
42. Wikipedia, *http://en.wikipedia.org/wiki/String_of_Pearls_(China),* accessed on 22 Feb 14
43. Wikipedia, ibid
44. Cdr KK Agnihotri, "Chinese Quest for a Naval Base in the Indian Ocean – Possible Options for China", Maritime Affairs, National Maritime Foundation, 08 Feb 2010.
45. Cdr KK Agnihotri, ibid.
46. *http://uk.reuters.com/article/2014/01/20/china-oil-demand-id UKL3 N0KQ2ZW20140120,* UPDATE 3-China's 2013 oil demand sees slowest rise in at least 22 years
47. ibid
48. "China's Oil Production Ranks 4th in World, Only Meets Half Domestic Demand," People's Daily Online, February 9, 2010. *http://english.peopledaily.com.cn/90001/90778/90860/6891500.html*
49. Frederic Vellucci Jr, "Extending the First Line of Defence: China's Naval Strategy and Development Prospects," PLA Navy Build Up and ROK Navy-US Navy Cooperation, Korean Institute of Maritime Strategy, June 2009, Session I, pp 237-286, p.267.
50. See You Ji, "Dealing with the Malacca Dilemma: China's Effort to Protect its Energy Supply", Strategic Analysis, 31 no. 3, p. 468.

51. "Chinese Navy urged to go from coastal waters to the oceans," *Xinhua*, 3 March 2009, available at *http://news.xinhuanet.com/english/2009-03/07/content_10963412.htm.*

52. "8th Chinese Naval Escort Taskforce Arrives in Gulf of Aden", PLA Daily website, Mar 16 2011. *http://eng. chinamil. com.cn/news-channels/china-military-news/2011-03/16/content_ 4404718.htm*

53. D. S. Rajan, The Unfolding China's Indian Ocean Strategy, Paper No. 5646, South Asia Analysis Group, 12 Feb 2014

54. D.S. Rajan, ibid

55. D.S. Rajan, ibid

56. *http://usnwc.libguides.com/content.php?pid=129699&sid=1112676,* accessed on 22 Feb 2014

57. See Business Monitor International, 10 Mar 2010. *http://usnwc.libguides.com/content.php?pid=129699&sid=1112676*

58. K.M. Panikkar, Índia and the Indian Ocean (London: Geaorge Allen & Unwin Ltd., 1945), p. 84.

59. Raja Menon and Rajiv Kumar, "The Long View from Delhi (New Delhi: Academic Foundation, 2010), p. 161.

60. Amit Kumar, "China's Island Strategy in the Indian Ocean: Breaching India's Sphere of Influence", *http://www. observer india.com/cms/sites/orfonline/modules/analysis/attachments/influence_1253251335478.pdf*

61. Amit Kumar, ibid

62. Jamie Hatcher, "China's Growing Indian Ocean Maritime Interests: Sowing the Seeds of Conflict?" Sea Power Center, Australia, October 13, No 2.

4

The Changing Paradigm of Sino-India Relationship

Rahul Kumar Seth

Introduction

India and China is the world most populous countries in the world lies in Asian continent. Both countries shares 3488 kilometres long border. The history of trade relation, religious flowering, diplomatic relations can be seen clearly in both countries. But after a war in 1962 situation were transformed. Many diplomatic analyst declares that China will be a big threat to India not Pakistan. Although India is the large importer of Chinese manufactured goods and the current Indian government were trying to keep healthy relationship with China in spite of these China through his expansion policy tries to obtain Indian territory in Arunachal Pradesh, Sikkim and Ladakh. If we talked about China's

Research Scholar, Defence & Strategic Studies, Tilakdhari PG College, Jaunpur UP Mob. 9026614316, E-mail: rahulsethp@gmail.com expansion policy then we will found that China wants to took advantage with Pakistan through its One Belt – One Road project. As we know that the technological development reduces the inaccessibility of high altitude terrainand the Himalaya is now irrelevantas a natural boundary. The border disputes are present between India and China was seeded by British because they left disputed International borders in this region. Through his expansion policy on 8th September 1959 China refuses to accept the McMahan line, stating that China was not a signatory to the 1842 peace treaty between British India and Tibet. This leads China claim 50,000 square miles of Indian territory in Sikkim and Bhutan. Recently the border dispute and military standoff in Ladakh territory change is the paradigm between these two countries.

A Comparative Perspective

Being a neighbour countries and ancient connectivity both countries have some similarities. Both are world's most populous country and fastest growing economy in the world. Both countries are connected with religious and cultural terms. Both country is connected with joint military exercises. Bilateral trade between China and India touched above $87 billion in 2018-19. India's export was nearby $16.7 billion and import was nearby $70.3 billion. On one side India followed a peace policy and become republic with mutual understanding and looking for better future, China's policy seen with aggression and established there communist government to war and suppression. Chinese economy is five times bigger than India and military is four times bigger. This year India and China complete their 70 years of diplomatic relationship which was founded in April 1950. On this occasion of celebrationwere planning, which includes many people to people, political and cultural events and objective was to open up the historical relationship between the two countries. But these events will not be possible due to current tension and scenario.

The first Annual Defence dialogue between two nations was conducted in Beijing in Nov, 2007. Indian side was led by Sri BimalJulka, JS (G/Air), Ministry of Defence (MOD) while the Chinese side was led by Major General Qian Li Hua, chief of Foreign Affairs Office (FAO) of the Ministry of National Defence (MND). The second round of Annual Defence Dialogue was held in India on 15 Dec, 2008. The third round of Defence Dialogue held in Beijng on 6th Jan, 2010. The Indian side was led by General Ma Xiaotian, Deputy Chief of General staff. The fourth Annual Defence dialogue was held in New Delhi in 9thDec, 2011. Sri Shasikant Sharma, Defence Secretary and Gen Ma Xiaotian, Dy CGS Co-chaired the talks. Both sides agreed to increase the defence exchanges between two countries and enrich the content of the exchanges. The important high level visit that took place from India to China in the year 2011 were by an India multi-command delegations led by Maj Gen Gurmit Singh, VSM from 19-23 Jun and 15 members staff officers delegations led by Air Marshal PS Mann from 09-14 Jan 2012. An eight member PLA delegations led by Lt Gen Lang Youliang, political commissar of Tibet provincial military command visited India from 04-09 Nov, 2011. Another 26 member PLA staff officer Delegations visited Delhi, Agra, and Mumbai, from 25-30 Dec 2011. It was headed by Maj Gen Jin Lecheng, Deputy Commander, Shanxi provincial military command. All exchanges are meant to deepen and institutionalize defence co-operations. The bilateral exchanges between two countries are increasing with defence delegations.

Present Stand off

Recently the Indian ministry of Home Affairs (MHA) has decided to spend 10% fund to Central sponsored scheme only on border projects in Ladakh, Arunachal Pradesh, Himachal Pradesh, Uttarakhand and Sikkim. And after the connectivity with remotes border area in Ladakh, near siachin and air strip at Daulat Beg Oldie (DBO), Chinese behaviour can be seen in present Ladakh region. The step taken by Chinese people is not new. In 2017 China-India border standoff referred as doklam standoff were seen at trijunction border area at doklam. In Ladakh region press stand-off is inspired by mainly two factors-

(a) Distract the words attention from covid-19.

(b) India built a strategic road which connect Let Durbuk Shyok to Daulat Beg Oldie.

Chinese people Liberation Army increase military resources near LAC and wants to pressurize India by conducting manoeuvres.

India's Stand

After analysing the current situation in Ladakh territory near LAC India's stand is clear that is-

(a) India cleared that, not accept less than status-quo-ante.

(b) India can build border infrastructure in his side or territory, it is the legal right.

Future Aspects

Both side of LAC a huge mistrust is seen, which can be dissolved through bilateral better communication. If necessary then involvement of third party also. If we carefully see the current situation then we found that India engaged in liberal and Panchsheel mind set. India affected with the policy of Hindu mind set strategy since ancient time. We are facing otheron own land whereas China do opposite term of India. The most geo-strategic Border Road Initiative project is also funded byAsian Infrastructure Investment Bank (AIIB) and the most investment in it by Indians. India have to take strong decision against the investment of Indian investors. In the Chinese perspective, the strategic and global dimension of India-China relation has week ended and bilateral issues have re gained silence. In recent exchanges,

Chinese academic advice India to acknowledge the changed and "unequal" power relations. China no longer sees the urgency of resolving the boundary issue to enhance the strategic dimension of India-China relations. The special representative dialogue has receded into the background even as Chinese activity at the line of actual control has increased. China is not actively seeking to advance its presence in countries in India's neighbourhood clearly evident in Nepal and Sri Lanka. China's relations with Pakistan have now gone beyond the letter's role as a proxy to constrain India. It is now a part of China's long-term and strategic initiative of One Belt-One Road. Sensitivity to India's confirm has diminished with China not only ceiling Pakistan on the issue of cross- border terrorism but also in blocking India's entry into the nuclear suppliers group. The one area that is still interest China is what president XI Jinping has referred to as a development partnership between India and China. This could potentially become a new era of convergence as a growing Indian economy become a significant opportunity for a China whose economy is slowing and excess capacity continuous to mount.

Conclusion

Although China is big economic power than India but India can not left their geo-strategic conditions. India needs to rethink about his relationship with China. It is also very clear that the present standoff in Ladakh territory will not be resolve soon. It is a condition of wait and watch. So for keeping future aspects it is the time when India get advantage of the world's condition against China through multi lateral partnership with those countries who are reconsidering their relationship with China. Undoubtedly China want to do something according to his deep thinking long term policy. It is also a big truth that the mistrust which had been created will not be easily dissolve and not trust by close eyes because it was the policy of China since ancient times that make noise in East and attack to West.

References

1. Bhaghel, Dr.Virendra Singh, Rashtriya Suraksha Ke Samaksh Chunautiyaan
2. Donnell, Frank O, The Strategic Posture of China and India A visual Guide
3. Kumar, Ashok, Internal Security of India: Challenges
4. Ratha, KeshabChandra and Mahapatra, Shushanta Kumar, Research Journal, India-China Bilateral Relations: Confrontation and Conciliation
5. Saran, Shyam, Changing Dynamics in India China relationship, Article, The Hindu
6. *https://www.google.com/amp/s/www.bhaskar.com/amp/db-original/news/url-india-china-relation-latest-news-70-years-of-diplomatic-relations-anniversary-all-you-need-to-know-127441758.html*
7. *https://www.tandfonline.com/doi/abs/10.1080/00358530410001679602?journalCode=ctrt20*
8. *https://www.google.com/amp/s/theprint.in/diplomacy/1954-panchsheel-pact-to-galwan-valley-violence-india-china-relations-in-last-7-decades/442810/%3famp*
9. *https://thediplomat.com/2020/06/the-origins-of-todays-sino-india-tensions/*
10. *https://en.m.wikipedia.org/wiki/China%E2%80%93India_relations*
11. *https://navbharattimes.indiatimes.com/opinion/editorial/india-china-border-dispute-to-be-prolonged/articleshow/76277791.cms*
12. *https://www.drishtiias.com/hindi/daily-updates/daily-news-editorials/india-china-relations-challenges-and-emerging-issues*

5

Tibet: An Appraisal

Lt Gen R.C. Chadha

Introduction

Tibet covers an area of about 2.5 million sq km indeed a very vast, but 75% of this is largely inhabited because of extreme climate. It is located between 28 and 38 degrees North parallels and 78 and 103 East meridian. Tibet is appropriately called the 'Roof of the world" since it is the highest and the broadest plateau inthe world, ranging between 16000 and 11000 ft in height. Mountains remain covered for most part of the year, by thick mantle of snow, with lowest temperatures touching minus 40degree Celsius in the winter. The area is rich in metals and minerals like gold, iron, copper, coal, tungsten, uranium, manganese, tin, etc which can make the country extremely rich, if properly exploited.

Tibet is closely associated to India as its royal dynasty started from a descendent of ruler of Magdha who was

Director General, Operation Logistic, New Delhi

exiled from India. He became the ruler of Yarlung in 127 BC and was named as Nyatra Tsanpo. The Indo Tibetan relationship had always been cordial. Buddhist spiritual leader Shantarakshita established the monastery "Samyas Migyar Lhungi Dubpai Tsukla-khang" on the request of then King Trisong Delsen. The Sino-Tibetan relations were always bitter. Tibetans defeated China decisively in the year 763 and dominated it for almost 20 years there on. However, after several reversals, China emerged as strong power and claimed Tibet to be an integral part of Peoples Republic of China. Tibetan Government has been in exile in India since 1959. Tibet always served as a buffer state between British administered India and China. India provided asylum to large number of Tibetans and the Dalai Lama in the 50's.[1]

Chinese viewed Aksai Chin as a strategically important area to maintain their supply lines to Tibet. Delhi knew little about these remote parts of Ladakh as is evident from the fact that Xinjiang–Tibet Road was discovered by India only after it was written about in a Chinese Magazine in 1957. India officially claimed Aksai Chin in a note to·Chinese Ambassador in Delhi in Oct 1958. India officially objected to inclusion of Northern Assam and NEFA (now Arunachal Pradesh) in China pictorial in Sep 1958. Thou Enlai spelt out China's Claim to over 40000 sq miles of Indian Territory in Ladakh and NEFA in Jan 1959. Beijing also laid claims to 5000 square miles of territory in Sikkim and Bhutan. China occupied another 12000 square miles in the Western Sect in Feb 1961. On Sep 08, 1962, 800 Chinese Soldiers surrounded Indian Post at Dhola but neither side opened fire for 12 days. Chinese offensive overran inadequate Indian Defences in five days commencing Oct 20, 1962 both in Ladakh and NEFA. The second offensive in mid–November was even more furious when in four days flat China delivered humiliating defeat.

In the recent past, the PLA has created infrastructure

in Tibetan plateau which have enhanced the threat to India. In the period from 1950-99, the Chinese Government spent over Yuan 40 billion on construction activities and financial subsidies for Tibet. The increased frequency of PLA training exercises in Tibet, improvements in military infrastructure as well as improvements in the weapons and equipment for high altitude and mountain warfare, the operational readiness of PLA has been tremendously enhanced.

China has settled boundary issues with virtually all countries with which it had disputes except India. The Northern borders of India with Tibet were based on MacMohan Line as the boundary which the Chinese did not recognize as the borders with India. China had laid large territorial claims in the Indian territorial claims in the Ladakh region, Himachal Pradesh, hills of Uttar Pradesh (now Uttarakhand), the whole of the then North East Frontier Agency (NEFA)(now called Arunachal Pradesh) and Sikkim (Sikkim was an Indian Protectorate).

China's Interests/Objectives

National Interests

The 12th Communist Party Congress in 1982 for the first time in the history of the People's Republic of China (PRC) specifically mentioned 'National Interests.' State Councillor Dai Binggou's statement (July 2009) on China's core interests included the Maintenance of its Fundamental System and State Security, Preserve and Promote the Legitimacy of Chinese Communist Party(CPC), Protection of State Sovereignty and Territorial Integrity and Stable Development of the Economy and of the Society. The issues of importance are:-

(a) Development of heartland and to address the concerns over inequality and the consequent perception of 'Relative Sense of Deprivation' in minds of the agriculturist heartland.

(b) Control non- Han Buffer through economic development and social re-engineering (Sinocitisation) and simultaneously combat the three evils of extremisms, separatism and terrorism.

(c) Assimilate Taiwan, reclaim the claimed islands and dominate the EEZ in the East and South China seas.

(d) Control access to resources and markets; protect the coastline and SLOCs.

(e) Expansion of politico-economic and military influence over Asia-Pacific and the regional periphery[2].

Strategic Objectives

As per China's white papers, China seeks to be the 'Sole Asian Power' by 2020 and become a great Power by 2050 and this assertion is reinforced by Xi Jinping in his China Dream Slogan. Ingredients of this assertion are:-

(a) Noteworthy growth in its key national endeavours.

(b) Inducing Asian states to perceive stability, development and security under the Chinese leadership.

(c) China so far has displayed a propensity to use her military to challenge and contest other Asian as well as extra regional powers. She believes it has militarily challenged USA, India and Vietnam and even now is demonstrating her newly created military capabilities. China would look for windows of opportunity to designate Vietnam, Japan or India as an erring state(s). The Chinese Government frequently states that stability and development in Tibet is the foundation for its long term well-being. They have deployed a large number of troops all across Tibet. Tibetans live in constant fear and anxiety.

Development of Infrastructure

By 1965, two highways effectively linked Lhasa with interior China. By1975, China had completed 91 highways totalling 15,800 Km, with 300 permanent bridges in Outer Tibet alone, by which 97 per cent of the region's counties were connected by roads[3]. The robust and extensive rail and road network built on Tibet plateau is meant for economic exploitation of natural resources and for speedy induction and deployment of military forces for both internal and external contingencies.

Roads

The total length of roads in TAR is presently 51000 kms and all major highways have been upgraded to class 50 specifications. The highway from Kashgar and Lhasa is 3105 km. The CentralHighway connects Gormo to Lhasa and is 1154 kms, class 50, two way, black top road with a capacity of 5100 tons per day.

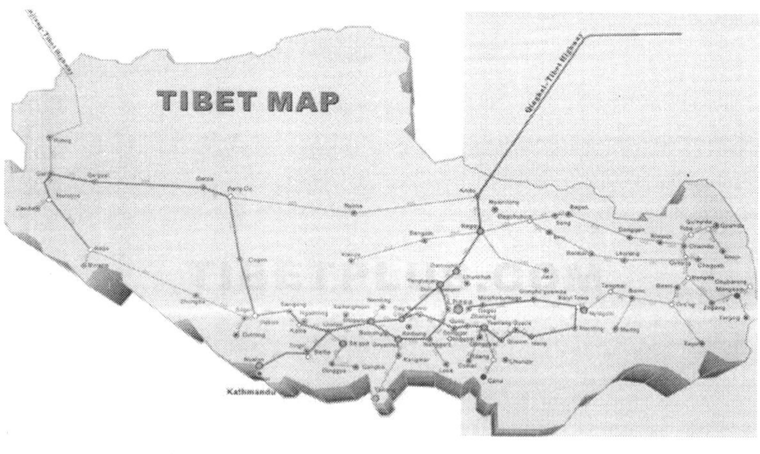

Source: Tibettravel.com

The Eastern Highway connects Chengdu to Lhasa and is 1715 kms long, class 50, two way,black top road with a capacity of 3200 tons per day. On the Central Highway, a

90-km stretch between Lhasa and Yangbaja in has been developed as a four-lane highway. With these improvements, the assessed capacity of the highways in the TAR is estimated to be 7,100 tonnes per day[4].

Railway

The Qinghai – Tibet Railway (QTR) has almost become a lifeline of Tibet. China has already built settlements with Han population every 60 km of this vital 1,118 km long railway. This population is settled with the intention of monitoring, repairs and reconstruction of railway in case of disruption by the subversive elements. China has employed helicopter for sky patrols and aerial photography over this link. QTR has enhanced theability to quickly manoeuvre the equipment and movement of Chinese nuclear forces. China is able to readily transfer intermediate and intercontinental range ballistic missiles to the Indian border, if needed. The Golmud-Lhasa route stretches from Nanshankou in Golmud city (Qinghai province) to Lhasa via Nachitai, Xidatan, Kunlun Mountain, Chumar River, Tanggula Mountain, Amdo, Cona, Nagchu, Sangxiong, Nayake, Damxung, Ningzhong, Yangbaijin Canyon and Deqen. Southward extension of the QTR connects two most important cities of Tibet ie Lhasa and Xigaze. The plan to connect Nyingchi is also on anvil, Nyingchi is strategically important as China proposes to divert Bramhaputra at the Great Bend (where Bramhaputra turns towards India) by constructing the largest dam in the World. The rail link to Nyangtri has been described as a significant new development. China has unveiled plans to construct the world's largest damwhich will be more than twice bigger than Three Gorges Dam, now the world's largest dam, and also because it will strengthen China's rapid military deployment capability in the Eastern (Arunachal) Sector.

516 km of rail lines are in the TAR and 564 km of railway is in Qinghai Province. More than 960 km (out of 1132 km) is above an altitude of over 13000 feet. The railway

line has been constructed in areas where winter temperatures are as low as minus forty degrees Celsius. The rail line passes through thirty tunnels and bridges, covering a total distance of 37.5 km, and run parallel to the Golmud-Lhasa Highway. QTR gives China the capability tomobilise up to 12 divisions in a month's time frame. Reliable rail links from Lanzhouto Kashi and Lhasa also facilitate easy switching of reserves and logistic resourcesbetween Chengdu and Lanzhou MRs reducing the travelling time for troops from Golmud to Lhasa from approximately 72 hoursto merely 16 hours. 30 Regiments of PLA stationed at Golmud can use the railway line and reach Lhasa, Xigaze and other feeder lines. The Chengdu - Lhasa line can bring in five more PLA divisions to the border

The other railway projects are:-

(a) **Gansu-Tibet Railway.** The railway would extend from Yongjin County near Lanzhou in Gansu Province to Lhasa via Guanghe, Hezhi, Linxia, Dari, Shiqu, Yushu, Sog County and Nagchu to join the above mentioned Qinghai-Tibet Railway.

(b) **Sichuan– Tibet Railway.** This extends from Dujiangyan close to Chengdu in Sichuan Province to Lhasa via Markang in Aba, Jinshajiang River, Gyangda, Lancangjiang River, Bome and Yunnan-Tibet Highway. In addition,

China has built a 1142 km long electrified railway line from Golmud (Gormo in Tibetan language) to Lhasa and has plans to extend the line to Shigatze and Yatung, reaching almost till the strategic Nathu Lapass. China is planning to extend the Golmud-Lhasa (Qinghai Tibet) railway line to Nyingchiclose to its border with India on the Arunachal Pradesh side and further extend it to Dali in Yunnan Province. This line, running parallel to Arunachal Pradesh, will enable the PLA to rapidly relocate troops stationed in Kunming, Dali and Kaiyuanand to

> TAR. It also enablesthe 13 Group Army to relocate from Sichuan Province to TAR. It has reduced the travelling time from mainland China to Lhasa to two days with a total tonnage capacity of 3,200 tonnes per train.

It is also well known that the robust and extensive rail and road network built on Tibet plateau is meant for economic exploitation of natural resources and for speedy induction and deployment of military forces for both internal and external contingencies. In its current Five Year Plan (2011-2015), China would be extending rail line from Lhasa to Shigatse (opposite Sikkim) and to Nyingchi town (closer to Arunachal Pradesh border). Extension of rail to Kathmandu is also on the anvil. A division sized force requiring 20 trains of various configurations can thus be moved along the QTR to Lhasa in three days time.

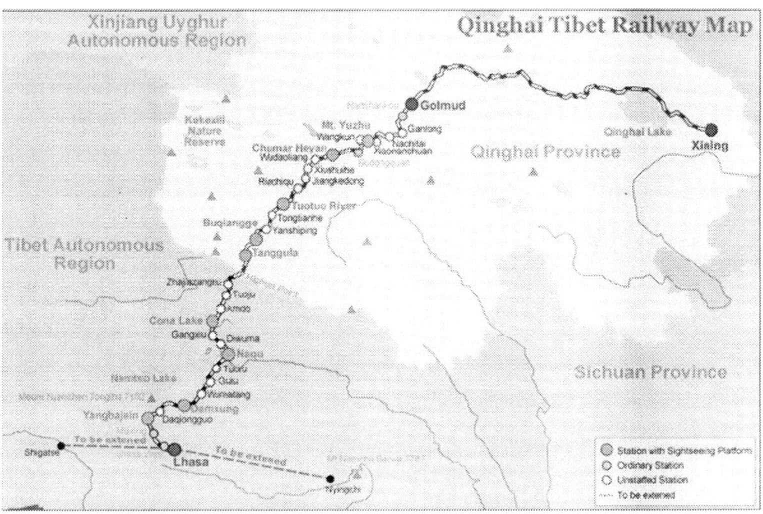

Source: *http://www.chinatibettrain.com/tibet-trian-map-htm*

Airfields/Airports

The main airfields in Tibet are at Gongga, Donshoon, Hoping, Bangda, Nagchuka and Shiquanhe. The five civil airports operating for civil activity are Lhasa, Bangda (Qamdo

Prefecture), Nyigtri, Gunsa(Ngari Prefecture) and Xigade. The Chinese leadership has recently remarked that both the Army and regional Civilian authorities should pool resources in the preparation for military struggle (against

China's enemies) indicating that the civilian infrastructure created in the frontier provinces of Tibet and Xinjiang has been also designed to strengthen national defence capabilities.

Oil and Gas Pipeline

With the simultaneous completion of the railway and road infrastructure, the PRC is building and linking the Qinghai oil and gas field with Lhasa through a gas/oil pipe line as part of their 12th Plan.

CAINONET

China's Advanced Info-Optical Network (CAINONET) project aims atconnecting this area with the mainland through an extensive optical fiber cable network. Inaddition, 58 Very Small Aperture Terminal (VSAT) satellite stations are part of the robustcommand and control structure in Tibet.[5] Broadband connectivity and secure means of communications between successive higher headquarters, including Lanzhou and Chengdu Military Region, have been developed.

Nyingchi Golden Tourist Complex

As part of new developments in border areas, China is building a "golden" tourist complex in the Nyingchi prefecture which is close to India. The Guangdong province in the South of China is earmarked to invest 400 million Yuan ($63.5million) for this purpose at the behest the central government in Beijing. An additional investment of two billion Yuan ($317 million) is expected to flow into Nyingchi from different enterprises once it develops as a tourist destination[6]. These developments will provide directaccess to the PLA basednear the Indian borderand moreover serve to provide scope for surreptitious moves and mobilization of forces.

Water Hegemony

China's policy of using water as a strategic asset emanates from a deficit of the same in the mainland. The dominant status that itenjoys from being an upper riparian state controlling Tibet, the "water tower of Asia", accords special significance to the use of this asset. This geographic advantage can be exploited by diverting trans-border rivers (Indus and Brahmaputra) and building dams China has not shared hydrological data with lower riparian states.

Operational Effects

In operational terms, China is building arailhead close to the LAC. There also exists a subsidiary road axis to the forward areas in Tibet. Of the 31 major passes, 28 have motorable roads and the remaining also being developed. In the Central Sector, 23 passes are connected by all-weather roadsto the hinterland. Development of infrastructure in Tibet provides the PLA adequate capacityto support the existing level of military presence, as well as cater for additional forces up to five Group Armies. This infrastructure provides logistic flexibility to China's Armed Forces. In addition, camps with living accommodation, warehouses and hardstandings have been created in a large number of areas which can support the operations of Armed Forces. A network of new camps and barracks with facilities for rapid acclimatisation of troops gives the Chinese an enhanced capability to employ accretional forces from other regions with lower attitudes.

The PLA General Logistics Department isassessed to be capable of transporting 5-6 million tons annually into

Tibet[7]. This is adequate for all types of requirements including the logistic support for a major military campaign. The PLA troops remain acclimatized as the military camps are established close to the border (these are not cantonments). On the other hand acclimatisation before deployment becomes a major challenge for the Indian troops. China is capable of mobilising an additional 100,000 troops from the Central Reserve within six weeks.

Command, Control, Communications, Intelligence, Surveillance and Reconnaissance (C4ISR)

For over a decade the PLA has been concentrating on giving a practical shape to its doctrine of fighting Local Wars under the Conditions of Informalisation. China has vastly improved its C4ISR capabilities and has laid out a vast network of underground fibre optic communication lines for secure means of communications and enhances its information warfare capabilities. Launching of several military satellites and placing them in space has enabled the PLA to provide force multiplication to its ground assets. 58 Very Small Aperture Terminal (VSAT) satellite stations are part of the robust command and control structure in Tibet[8]. Broad-band connectivity and secure means of communications between successive higher HQs including Lanzhou and Chengdu Military Region back to Beijing.

The construction of the Lhasa Railway Oil Terminal Project began on 8th Jun 2010. The oil terminal will have an annual oil turnover of 400,000 tons. China has created the biggest logistics centre in the TAR in Jun 2009 in Nagqu in Northern Tibet, next to a railway station at an altitude of 4,500 meters. This is likely to handle 2.23 million tonnes of cargo by 2015 and 3.1 million tonnes by 2020. 34 Since the centre is situated about 300 km Northeast of Lhasa. The infrastructure development in TAR builds Chinese capacity of transporting men and material to critical sectors on the Northern and Eastern borders; as also, it provides the Chinese a transportation infrastructure to open upTibet's market. It will speed up induction timings, increase buildup and logistic sustenance capability as well as night movement will also be possible by train. New townships, built-up complexes and barracks/buildings along the highways could be used for stocking of material thus enhancing force sustenance for longer durations.

Implications For India

China and India though geographical neighbours do not enjoy cordial relations. TAR, as per Chinese claims, includes many parts of India and Bhutan. Arunachal Pradesh though administrated as a state by India is claimed by China as a part of the Tibet Autonomous Region (TAR). Chinese also had claims on the Bhutan territory especially the areas with Sikkim. The boundary between India and China runs along the "MacMahon Line" in the Himalayas based on the "Watershed Principle". China has reorganised its ground forces into group armies. The creation of the elite Rapid Response Force, composed of troops belonging to Scouts, Infantry, Artillery, Signals, Engineers, Anti-Chemical Warfare and airborne fighters has substantially upgraded the overall military capability. These are highly technology-based forces. A diaspora of over 100,000 Tibetans, mostly well educated and politically aware, with Dalai Lama providing a focus, are viewed by China with grave suspicions. This affects and blocks the progress on the border settlement and withdrawal of territorial claims by China. China even fears that India might itself become a base for the subversive activities of the Dalai Lama's supporters. Consequently, China believes that its aggressive posture on Arunachal Pradesh will deter India.

Conclusion

The infrastructural development in TAR gives China militarystrategic operational flexibility, enhances their offensive capability against India throughout the year. Stocking capability which was limited to 4-5 months in a year, will no more be a restricting factor. China is capable of speedily inducting the armed forces, using five highways, railways and air infrastructure up to the major townships in TAR. It is in the Indian interest to upgrade the logistics infrastructure in the states bordering China. A capability to rapidly build up forces in threatened sector is imperative. Simultaneously, India should enhance its intelligence, surveillance and reconnaissance (ISR) capabilities. The Army and the Air Force must also upgrade their firepower capabilities so as to engage PLA forces at long distances.

References

1. History of Tibet by Tashi Delek on *http://www.tibetan-alliance.sorg/history of_tibet.html*
2. Chapter one of "The War Waging Potential of China-2025" by research team sponsored by Directorate of Net Assessment, HQ IDS (MoD).
3. Chapter five of "A History of Tibet" by SP Gupta and KS Ramachandran.
4. Lhasa and its Mysteries with a record of the expedition of 1903-1904 published by K M Mittal, Sanskaran
5. China Advance Info-Optical Network by Heqing Yi Jianguo Yu
6. Strategic Posture of China In Tibet Autonomous Region And Its Implications: Is India Prepared? by Gen (Retd) NC Vij
7. 2011 Sustainable Development Report by Sinopec Corp.
8. Strategic Asia 2012-13 "China's Military Challenge" edited by Ashley J. Tellis and Travis Tanner

6

Bhutan-China Relationship and India's Strategic Interests

Dr. Ashutosh Pandey

The Treaty of 1949 has been a major contributor to bringing India and Bhutan's friendship closer. Under this treaty, Bhutan also has to involve India in the matter of its foreign relations. However, the agreement was amended in 2007 and it was added that Bhutan would inform them of the foreign affairs in which India would be directly involved. Not only this, the treaty will commit both countries to close cooperation with each other on issues related to their national interests and not to allow their territories to be used against each other's national security and interests. Therefore, this treaty between India and Bhutan has always knocked China. India also has influence on the financial and defense policy of Bhutan, a country of eight lakh population in the lap of Himalayas between India and China.

Associate Professor, Department of Political Science and Public Administration, Dr. Shakuntala Misra National Rehabilitation University, Lucknow U.P.

Not only this, Bhutan exports 98 percent of its exports to India and also imports about 90 percent of its goods from India itself. The Indian Army has been training the Royal Army of Bhutan. These things have also troubled China somewhere. This area is where the borders of Sikkim and Bhutan, present in the north-east of China and India, meet. Both Bhutan and China lay claim to the region and India supports Bhutan's claim. It is the same region that connects India with the North Eastern states known as Seven Sisters and is strategically very important. India shares a 699-km border with Bhutan. In 2001, India started the SASEK (South Asian Sub-Regional Economic Co-operation) corridor to connect Bhutan, Nepal, Bangladesh and Myanmar. The route connecting Imphal to Moreh (Myanmar) is considered to be India's gateway to the East Asian market. India plans to connect the East Asian markets to the northeastern states through this route has brought the project. With the construction of the Imphal-Moreh route, India will have an alternative route to reach Bangkok. Maldives and Sri Lanka also became members in 2014. India has brought this project in response to China's ambitious OBOR project. Himalayan country Bhutan lies between India and China. The presence of a country in the neighborhood of large nations in the world creates a very complex situation. Keeping its territorial integrity and sovereignty intact, intensified relations with India and pursued a path to further relations with China. Despite limited economic and military capabilities, Bhutan's unique political character never came under colonial influence and also protected itself from the direct effects of two world wars and the Cold War. Tibetan culture, Bhutan's geo-strategic importance in the region has increased significantly due to its deep contact with language and history, and the disputed relationship between China and Tibet. On the other hand, relations of Bhutan India have developed on harmony and understanding which has played an important role in introducing parliamentary democracy in Bhutan. Despite being an economically underdeveloped nation, Bhutan is paramount for India from a geopolitical point of view (especially due to India's location in the 'Chicken Neck Corridor' and the distance between Nepal and Bangladesh is also short). The disputed border with China also increases Bhutan's geo-strategic importance.

China's objectives were not only limited and short-lived in Bhutan until the 1960s, but the tension was not over as the border dispute was not resolved and remained so until Bhutan started the border talks with China in 1979.[1]

Long ago, Nepal and China have pursued their own interests by making India stand tall, while Bhutan has always stood in support of India. Initially, relations between Bhutan and China were problematic, in the map published in "A Brief History of China" in the year 1956, China showed its claim on many areas of Bhutan, which led to a long border dispute. This map shows that "an important region of Bhutan is the prehistoric region of China." In this context, India's Prime Minister Jawaharlal Nehru said in the Indian Parliament that "the entry into the Himalayan barrier is not acceptable to India and it is the responsibility of India to protect Bhutan, Nepal and Sikkim."[2] In the year 1950 itself, China "considered Bhutan one of the five fingers of the palm of Tibet."[3] Concerned Bhutan at this time resorted to Article 2 of the decade-old British Heritage India Bhutan Treaty of 1979, stating that "In this situation, the Government of Bhutan decided that it would follow the instructions on foreign affairs as per the advice of the Government of India."[4] In the year 480, another provocative statement came from China, in which a Chinese leader said that "Bhutanese, Sikkimese and Ladakhi constitute a joint family in Tibet." They have always been subjects of the motherland of Tibet and China. "They should once again be united and learn the lesson of communism.[5] Apart from this, the social relations and religious relations of Bhutan's political elite were related to Tibet. In this context, when Tibet became insensitive to the map of the world, it became a kind of existential crisis for Bhutan. This complication was further compounded when the persecution of Chinese persecution of Tibetan people and religious institutions came to light, as described by Tibetan refugees visiting Bhutan.[6] To gain control of this situation, Bhutan broke all ties with Tibet (also severed relations with China automatically) and closed the northern borders. After this crisis, China established its suzerainty over Tibet in the year 1950 and in the year 1962.After the Chinese initiative towards Bhutan and the end of the India-China War of 1962, the China-side group in Bhutan began to emerge in the ruling class.[7] This context reflects the aftermath of the Indo-China war where India felt unable to assure Bhutan of security and it was right for Bhutan to adopt a policy of 'equal friendship' with India and China.[8]

Attempts by China to establish direct relations with Bhutan in the late 1950s were unsuccessful. The main reason for this was China's policy towards Bhutan's spiritual birthplace Tibet. The unfavorable relations between India and China played an important role in increasing the distance between Bhutan and China. In the late 1980s, India-China relations started improving under the leadership of the Janata government of India, which also brought positive changes in relations between Bhutan and China. The normalization of relations between India and China created an atmosphere for direct contact between Bhutan and China. Developing relations with Bhutan is not the only goal for China. [9]China believes that its relationship with Bhutan is part of the 'Western Development Strategy', which will help Tibet regain its central position in the Himalayan region.[10]

Paradoxically as an incident, in the year 1979, China infiltrated Bhutan's land border, resulting in the two countries coming face to face.[11] This time Bhutan raised its voice through India on the basis of the Bhutan India Treaty of 1979, while China offered to resolve the issue in a bilateral manner. Initially, negotiations on the modalities of direct engagement between Bhutan China started in the year 1961 and the negotiations on the direct border dispute started in the year 1919.[12] The border between Bhutan and Tibet was not correctly marked. China tried to prove that India could not help in this border dispute by putting pressure on Bhutan by infiltration.[13] Bilateral negotiations between Bhutan and China officially began in the year 1979 to settle the border dispute, which is still ongoing. During this period, Bhutan authorities also noted activities such as road construction and movement on controversial land by China.[14] These activities continued despite goodwill arising from bilateral contacts between the two countries. When Bhutan raised its voice on this issue, China proposed an interim agreement to maintain the disputed border and peace.[15] Bhutan accepted this and at the time of the 12th round of border talks in Beijing on December 1949, the agreement between Bhutan and China on peace keeping and border area was signed. This agreement was important not in one but several ways. [16] This was the first bilateral agreement between Bhutan and China and the first legal document on the matter. China signed Bhutan for the first time and accepted Bhutan's status of sovereignty and independence. Article 1 of the agreement clearly states that the two sides will follow the idea that all big and small, weak and powerful nations will be equal and respect each other. On behalf of China, it was confirmed that it would fully respect Bhutan's territorial integrity, sovereignty and independence.

Despite the signing of the peace-keeping agreement, China continued to infiltrate Bhutan's soil, creating an atmosphere of fear. China has also been involved in road construction work in the disputed area in the years 2006 and 2009 and has infiltrated Bhutan's Chinese army posts along the Bhutan-China border many times. [17]

The recent conversations between the leadership of both

Bhutan and China have been significantly positive. The two countries are meeting in major international conferences and improving relations. During the United Nations Conference on Sustainable Development in Rio de Janeiro in 2012, the Prime Ministers of Bhutan and China met and the Prime Minister of China said on the occasion that 'China wants formal relations with Bhutan to be established, the boundary between the two countries Issues should be improved, exchanges in all the areas should be strengthened so that China Bhutan relations reach new dimensions'.[18] In the 23rd round of talks on the border between Bhutan and China on August 24, 2015, various aspects of multilateral relations were discussed. They shared many regional and international views, apart from mutual interests and concerns. More recently, the proximity of China and Nepal has grown strategically and commercially and China is also facing strategic challenges from its east coast. In such a situation, the important exercise of taking Bhutan into its inner circle is worth noting. Now it is entirely up to Bhutan how to counter this pressure of China and maintain a cordial relationship with its larger neighbors. Today's democratic Bhutan is striving for independent foreign policy as an important dimension of its sovereignty, in which its relations with India remain strong and balance with other powers including China. Bhutan also protects itself from the attraction of its north-east neighbor China by the desire of investment, because its relations with India have been very trustworthy. But China's expansionary policy after the Doklam incident has raised the challenges of border security for both countries. China is keen to establish formal diplomatic and economic relations with Bhutan and to some extent the people of Bhutan are also supporting trade and diplomatic relations with China. This may pose some other challenges for India in the times to come. India needs to work vigorously to address Bhutan's concerns, as increasing Chinese intervention in Bhutan threatens to undermine the foundations of India-Bhutan's strong bilateral relations. Bhutan's political stability is very important for

India's strategic and diplomatic strategy. Thus, it can be said that Bhutan has an effective edge in India's foreign policy through strategic interests in terms of India's China, energy diplomacy in South Asia, security of North East India, development of green economy and training of Bhutanese Buddhist students. Wants to take the policy of Neighbors First and that India succeeds in its cause.

References

1. Tilak Jha, "China and Its Peripheries: Limited Objectives in Bhutan," Issue Brief 233, August 2013, IPCS, *http://www.ipcs.org/pdf_file/issue/IB233-TilakJha-ChinaPeriphery-Bhutan.pdf.*
2. Surjit Mansingh, "China-Bhutan Relations," *China Report* (New Delhi), vol. 30, no. 2, 1994, p. 177.
3. SD Muni, "Bhutan Steps Out," *The World Today* (London), vol. 40, no. 12, December 1984, p. 516.
4. Ahsan, Syed Aziz-al and Bhumitra Chakma. "Bhutan's Foreign Policy: Cautious Self Assertion?" *Asian Survey* . (USA: University of California Press, 1993), pp. 1043-1054.
5. Center for Bhutan Studies, "Economic and Political Relations between Bhutan and Neighboring Countries." Monograph 12 April 2004, *http://www.bhutanstudies.org.bt/wp-content/ uploads / monograph / mono-Ecnmc-Pol-Rel-BtNghbrng.pdf.*
6. Leo E. Rose, "Bhutan's External Relations," *Pacific Affairs* (Vancouver), vol. 47, no. 2, Summer 1974, p. 195.
7. SD Muni, "Bhutan Steps Out," *The World Today* (London), vol. 40, no. 12, December 1984, p. 515
8. Mathew C Joseph, "China South Asia Strategic Engagements 2 - Bhutan China Relations," ISAS Working Paper, No. 157, August 23, 2012, Institute of South Asian Studies, National University of Singapore, p. 8, *http://www.isas.nus.edu.sg/Attachments/PublisherAttachment/ISAS_Working_Paper_157_-_Bhutan_-_China_23082012174042.pdf.*
9. Mathew C Joseph, "China South Asia Strategic Engagements

2 - Bhutan China Relations," ISAS Working Paper, No. 157, August 23, 2012, Institute of South Asian Studies, National University of Singapore, p. 9, *http://www.isas.nus.edu.sg/Attachments/PublisherAttachment/ISAS_Working_Paper_157_-_Bhutan_-_China_23082012174042.pdf.*

10. Thierry Mathou, "Tibet and its Neighbors: Moving towards a New Chinese Strategy in the Himalayan Region," *Asian Survey* (Berkeley), vol. 45, no. 4, July-August 2005, p. 388.
11. Dorji Penjore, "Security of Bhutan: Walking between the Giants," Journal of Bhutan Studies (Thimphu), vol. 10, Summer 2004, pp. 116–117.
12. Mathew C Joseph, "China South Asia Strategic Engagements 2 - Bhutan China Relations," ISAS Working Paper, No. 157, August 23, 2012, Institute of South Asian Studies, National University of Singapore, p. 9, *http://www.isas.nus.edu.sg/Attachments/PublisherAttachment/ISAS_Working_Paper_157_-_Bhutan_-_China_23082012174042.pdf.*
13. Dorji Penjore, "Security of Bhutan: Walking between the Giants," *Journal of Bhutan Studies* (Thimphu), vol. 10, Summer 2004, p. 117.
14. Ibid.
15. Thierry Mathou, "Tibet and its Neighbors: Moving towards a New Chinese Strategy in the Himalayan Region," *Asian Survey* (Berkeley), vol. 45, no. 4, July-August 2005, pp. 410-411.
16. S. Chandrashekharan, "Bhutan's Northern Border: China's Bullying and Teasing Tactics," Update No. 82, Note no. 564, 14 January 2010, South Asia Analysis Group, URL: http://*www.southasiaanalysis.org/%5Cnotes6%5Cnote564.html.*
17. "China, Bhutan Look to Establish Formal Ties," *Sino Daily*, June 22, 2012, *http://www.sinodaily.com/reports/China_Bhutan_look_to_establish_formal_ties_999.html.*
18. Press Release, MFA / BDA-8/115, August 26, 2015, Ministry of Foreign Affairs, Royal Government of Bhutan, *http://www.mfa.gov.bt/wp-content/uploads/2015/08/IMG_0002 .pdf.*

7

India-China Strategic Rivalry

Dr. Nand Kishor Kumar

Introduction

Richard Nixon in 1994 stated that "China's economic power makes US lecture about human rights imprudent. Within a decade, it will make them irrelevant. Within two decades, it will make them laughable. By then the Chinese may threaten to withhold MFN status from the US unless we do more to improve living conditions in Detroit, Harlem and South Central LA."[1] Looking at today's Chinese strategic stature in 2014, the aforesaid prophesy made by Richard Nixon about China seems to be appropriate. However, despite the fact that no such eminent prophecy was made for future growth of India, the significant status occupied by India over the last 65 years, ever since her independence in 1947, is not the product of strategic mercy by any super power, as USA did for China, but by virtue of its own

Former Head Department of Political Science, National Defence Academy. Pune, Maharashtra efforts, that too, in unfavorable scenario inside and outside India. It is, therefore, the fact that China has undoubtedly grown tremendously in all aspects of national power, but India is also not very far behind. In this background Indo-China relation needs to be analyzed and examined in the present context without being prejudiced, biased and influenced by anti-India so-called western/Indian scholars who have the tendency to underrate India in relation to China. Yes, India's strategic face is not as bright as that of China, but overall India's position is also not as grim and pessimist looking as such authors attempt to paint it. This paper attempts to focus the framework of strategic background of both India and China in context with their relationship and also to highlight the impact of their strategic rivalry on the vital national, regional and global interest.

Strategic Perception

Strategy has been defined as a Plan designed to achieve a particular long term aim. It is also an art of planning and directing military activity in a war or battle. According to Stuart Poore, "...the term strategy has traditionally been used to refer to the way that the military power is used by government in the pursuit of their interest. How are theses interest shaped? A strategic culture approach tackles this question by considering the relevance of cultural context in influencing strategic preferences."[2]

Colin S. Gray in his work *'Strategy and History: Essays on Theory and Practice'* has pointed out six principles of strategic culture:

a. Strategic behavior cannot be beyond culture

b. Adversity cannot cancel culture

c. Strategic culture is a guide to action

d. Strategic culture expresses comparative advantage

e. Strategic culture can be dysfunctional

f. Strategic culture can be variously categorized, such as nationality, geography, weapons and functions, simplicity and complexity, generation and grand strategy.[3]

As regards Chinese strategic culture in terms of aforesaid six principles, the general impression about China begins with Sun Tzu of China, authored the 'Art of War', sometime between the 8th and 5th century BC, 3-4 centuries earlier than our own Kautilya, who wrote the 'Arthshastra' during 4th - 3th century BC. Both wrote broadly about strategy. They discussed statecraft, diplomacy, relationship with other nations and a host of other topics in their respective books. The prevalence of 'strategic culture' in the two countries can be gleaned from the fact that Sun Tzu's strategic principles were continuously updated by subsequent Chinese strategists over the centuries to keep them relevant to the changing technologies and environment. Kautilya's Arthshastra has become the object of historical studies and no serious attempts were made either by the military analysts or other strategists to evaluate its practical applicability and pertinent to developmental changes in India. Basically a moderate strategic culture has been followed in India throughout its history unlike China. The near absence of an aggressive strategic culture in India is further driven home if one scrolls down any listing of military strategists/writers over time. While Chinese names are like Jiao Yu, Shen Kuo, Sun Bin, Sun Tzu, Wu Qi, Liu Zi, Wang Xiangsui, Zhuge Liang and Mao Zedong, where as the only Indian in this list is Kautilya. China's push to become a global power is based on modern interpretation of Sun Tzu's classic and Chinese scholars rely on historical strategic lessons and 'Art of War' to develop strategy of the Chinese state and its leaders. In contrast, the strategic lessons India has learnt from its previous wars or international engagements.

The contrasting strategic cultures of China and India have strongly influenced bilateral relations in the past. The relations between the two countries will always have elements of competition and contest. Many international relations always maintain that given their geographical proximity and sheer sizes, China and India are natural rivals. Nancy Jetley, in her analysis of Sino-Indian relations, in an article written in 1992 stated that, "It needs to be clearly recognized that China's claims to vast territory of India are related in the main to ideological intent. The Chinese strategy, as it unfolded after 1959 was designed not so much to gain possession of a few thousand square miles of mountainous territory – not all of which are strategically vital to China – as to eliminate India as a power of consequence from the Asian scene. China's policy in South Asia – imposing deep national humiliation on India by exposing its strategic shortcomings in 1962, tarnishing its image as a great Asian country, systematically eroding its special ties with its Himalayan neighbors, exploiting sub-continental dissensions by embarking on a deliberate poly of collusion with Pakistan and above all weakening the political stability of India through its clandestine support to Mizo and Naga insurgents – has been essentially an exercise in isolating India and eroding its influence in the region." India regained some of its stature displaying superior military strategy in 1971.[4]

Following aggressive strategy by China and a moderate strategy of Five Principles – policy of peaceful co-existence and others (Panchshee) – followed by India, is a subject of serious analysis separately. What is gain/loss of such strategies of China and India is a matter of perception and national objectives as well as strategic goal. Hence India's strategic perception cannot be undermined without doing proper analytical study by unbiased strategists.

The western author like George Tanham stated that "India has not had a tradition of strategic thinking ….."[5] Further he said "Indians seem to arrive at strategic concept and decision rather than by thinking about them and then making a conscious decision."[6] Tanham is perhaps not familiar with complexities inherent to the Indian culture. Hence it is harder to trace out for him that there is a systematic strategic thought propounded by Manu (700 BC), Kautilya (300-400 BC), Ved Vyas and epics like Ramayan, Geeta, Mahabharata, Purans, Vedas etc in the past and subsequently Gandhiji, Subhash Bose, Ambedkar, Nehru, Indira, Rajeev, Bajpai, Savarkar, Shivaji etc. Unfortunately, many numbers of Indian authors, without applying their own reliable resources, blindly follow Tanham.

Whatever is said by western scholar, we have the habit of saying yes without verifying the fact. Tanhanm, if he is not known to the Indian culture, it could be understood as he is outsider, but how can we do it while living all the time in this culture. Scholars like Francine R. Frankel, Harry Harding, Susan L. Shirk, Stephen Cohen etc. argue that China hardly bothers for India. For China, India merits little attention and, even after India's May 1998 nuclear test, is not taken seriously as a security threat. China does not even consider India as one of the significant power in the world. India is simply not on China's "radar screen".[7] China's smug attitude toward India is not just a pose adopted in official statements for international purpose; it is reflected domestically as well. India has many more experts on China than China has experts on India. Indian policy toward China are broadly debated and handled at the highest level of political leadership, in contrast to Chinese policy toward India, which are ignored by the public and managed by the diplomats and bureaucrats. China's indifference to India and its disdainful, patronizing attitude toward India, infuriate the Indians.

Steven A. Hoffmann has highlighted India's view on China.[8] For India, China looms large as an economic and political rival and also as a security threat. However, India is self confident that it has potential to grow as a world power by means of its territorial/population size, economic strength, information technology, nuclear power, military muscles, skillful diplomacy, balance of defence and development, independent foreign policy, active participation in global affairs – UNO, WTO etc., democracy and Rule of Law, Independent judiciary, qualified man power with command of English language etc. Therefore, this is an illogical/mythical perception that India stands nowhere before China in term of strategic culture. The fact, as described above, that both China and India are very rich in strategic culture since last almost 3000 years. A part from it both shares a number of attributes. Exceptionally large population, sharing a 4,700 km long border, huge continental size, old civilization, culture and a history of invasions, internal turmoil and foreign exploitation are some of the major similarities. Even in their post – II World War history, both suffered from widespread poverty, dependence on agriculture, natural calamities, social and financial inequalities and a myriad other impediments to national development.

Their approaches to national security, however, are completely different. China chose to send its armies to 'liberate' Tibet, and entered the Korean War in support of North Korea, which was clearly the aggressor, India chose to go to the UNO when it was attacked by Pakistan in J&K.[9] China possessed nuclear weapon in 1964 despite Soviet Union's Security umbrella over China, when India felt that possession of nuclear weapon was immoral and asserted for total disarmament. Even if India tested nuclear capability in 1974 for peaceful purpose, it did not produce weapon. Besides, Chinese solders frequently violating LOC with India and objecting/humiliating Indians from Arunachal and J and K to visit China on normal visa. Chinese aggressive approach and India's moderate outlook, based on their respective cultures being followed for centuries, is the main point of difference in terms of strategic culture between the two.

In 1931 during Manchurian crisis, Indian National Congress (INC) supported China. In 1937 when Japan attacked main land of China, not only INC accused Japan, but also sent medical mission to China as a token of good gesture. Moreover, India is the second noncommunist country in the world which recognized communist China as a legitimate representative of China despite the fact that entire western countries recognized Taiwan instead of Communist China. Taiwan was not only an ordinary member of UNO but also the permanent member of Security Council of the UNO till 1970 when it was replaced by communist China with the western support. India, despite 1962 humiliation, kept raising Chinese (PLC) issue in UNO so that it could become the member of UNO before 1970.

China has been using Pakistan to contain India. India, following tit for tat, could have also easily taken support of Taiwan, South Korea and Japan against China; it did not do it keeping in mind its standard of diplomacy. However, India, despite being moralist, is conscious of national security and other vital national interest. 'Look east' policy brings India closure to Japan, South Korea, Myanmar, Bangladesh, Vietnam and other member of ASEAN as well as other countries in Asia Pacific, South East Asia and South Asia to counter China at its door. Hence, the views of anti-India scholars are not at all updated in terms of strategic tradition. If India is as weak as they claim it would have been collapsed as a nation immediately after partition of Pakistan, Pak attack in 1948, 1965 and Chinese attack in 1962. The fact is that India now is one of the 6 most significant nations in the world in terms of national power. Along with India, almost 2/3 countries of the world got independence after World War II and many of them subsequently collapsed or lost independence for one or the other reasons. Besides, only a very few of such survived countries now stand with true democracy like India. However, it is not a miracle or someone's unethical blessings behind the growth of India but by dint of its relevant strategy, policy and planning to operate state machinery, will to survive in the critical juncture of domestic and external hindrances, consensus approach in the diversity of culture and the art of management of coalition governance at the centre, and above all, a consistent self confidence, tolerance and a dynamic foreign and security policy.

What views China has about India, it is concerned to China as it is entitled to have it, but as scholars look that, it does not bother India despite the fact that India has respect for China that it is a great nation during past and present too. India is aware of its destination and the means to achieve it and it does not care what others think about it.

Strategic Framework

India

The strategy of China that Susan L. Shirk and Frankel talk about is not suited to Indian Strategic culture. China follows strategy of war, aggression, intervention, attack, occupation, belligerence, offence, invasion etc. Such concept of strategy is almost similar to the western one, imperialist, expansionist etc. India is very much clear about it. It has no intention of attacking others by initiating war, aggression or intervention or even proxy war as it respects the sovereignty of others. That is why it carries out Panchshil – the Five Principles-, Peaceful co-existence, non-aggression, non-intervention, non-alignment, non-apartheid, anti-colonialism, anti-racialism, anti-imperialism etc. Basically India is defensive in approach as regards its security policy is concerned.

But it does not mean that it would not retaliate in case it is attacked. It fights out against the aggressor by all means. Initially in the beginning of its independence it continued her faith on the goodness of Pakistan, China and others. India being a newly independent country followed the priority of 'development over defence'. As a result it suffered due to attack by Pakistan and China in 1948 and 1962 respectfully. Taking lesions from it, immediately after 62 debacles India by adopting a new strategy of 'the balance of defence and development,' it reorganized her new face that the world had seen absolutely a different India in 1965 and 1971 wars. Subsequently the nuclear test in 1974 and 1998, IPKF involvement in Sri Lanka, Army operation in Maldives, annexation of Sikkim, Kargil conflict etc. are the instances of India's strategic strength. Watching a tough face of India, her enemies understood the strategic reality of a strong nation. Now they do not dare to repeat the history of 1948 or 1962. Is it a weak India or is it the absence of strategic culture? India follows the strategy of the 'balance of armed forces and diplomacy'. These two elements of national power - a strong military forces and the skillful diplomacy - are cleverly utilized by India to protect her border and to promote her external national interest respectfully. 'Dynamism and flexibility' as an approach of her strategic outlook and its emphasis on 'humanity and morality' based on India's centuries old strategic culture ensure her solid road towards strategic success. 'No First Attack' in conventional warfare and 'No First Use of Nuclear Weapon' are the policy of long term strategic framework of India that is seriously carried out in practice and it is not merely a show-piece of strategic face, nor it is a sign of weakness of her strategy. India is a land of Mahatma Gandhi who believed that the 'peace and non-violence are an arms of braves, not of cowardice'. Gandhi's concept of peace and non-violence is not negative in approach as in case of Mahbeer Jain's thought. This is a dynamic strategy propounded by Gandhi that is followed by India during freedom struggle and also after independence. The peace based strategy is a long term means of national outlook depending upon the situation and circumstances. When Pakistan attacked on Kashmir, India sent armed forces to save Kashmir with Gandhi's blessings/support. It is, therefore, pacific means –

negotiation, conciliation, third-party approach, judicial/ arbitration/tribunal means etc. is followed till it is succeeding to achieve strategic goal. If it fails to realize national strategic target, India does not hesitate to shift to another option like muscles power/offensive means etc. depending upon the situation.

The Geeta, Mahabharat, Ramayan etc. - the great century's old Indian epics- teach an art of war and the principles of strategy. Lord Krishna, the great architect of war theory, encouraged Arjun in Geeta that attack the enemy vigorously in the battle field, whoever be the enemy, and forget about the result of war (karmanye wadhikaraste ma falesu kadachanam) However, he stressed upon the war for justice, not the war for unjust and immoral aspirations. Perhaps, this teaching of Geeta had motivated Indira Gandh to go for the most difficult war in 1971, despite a clear US nuclear threat on India, which finally ensured unprecedented victory in the world history. While fighting this war India still maintained her commitment for 'no first attack' and 'non-intervention'. The fact remains in this context that first Pakistan initiated war on western frontier of India and entered into Indian territory, which led Indian armed forces to retaliate in the eastern frontier on East Pakistan. Hence Indian retaliation was fully justified even from the views and norms of international law - Right to Preservation- apart from following India's own commitment for war strategy.

Nehru's style of security and foreign policy has been the subject of criticism – particularly his policy on Kashmir and China. Most of such critics are either politically motivated or biased or ill-informed. Some other critics, in this context, blame him for being idealist, as a result India suffered. However, this fact is ignored by such critics that both Pakistan and China directly and the western powers indirectly were aware that if India goes uninterrupted even for 10 – 15 years in the beginning of independence, it would be impossible for them to prevent it from growing as regional and global power. Nehru was not unaware of their intentions. Hence, he preferred small sacrifice for the sake of national and political stability and sovereignty. And he succeeded in facing initial storm and saved the nation from well architected conspiracy made by them jointly or separately. Nehru's decision to put up Kashmir problem to UNO, his acceptance of Tibet as part of China and following non-alignment is said to be his tactical move to keep up Indian flag flying at a critical juncture. It is argued that had he not succeeded in plying his shrewd move at that stage of strategically adverse situation, India could have paid very heavy price. Yes, Nehru's move seems to be following idealism but sometimes such approach of idealism is more suitable for the protection of national interest rather than realism propounded by Morgenthau. A nation like India that believes in dynamism in application of suitable policy, has faith in such a ideology which insists on balancing idealism and realism in the area of security and foreign policy. Extreme of either of the two is sometime disastrous for the nation. Nehru was well known and versatile master in dealing with such affairs, and hence he succeeded in leading the nation by defusing the crisis tactfully and took India out of the critical phase. Hence such argument looks a complete picture from untraditional angle and concludes that Nehru was not at all at the extreme of idealism but was a practical one in his approach in dealing with his assignment that the nation had entrusted on him.

Indira Gandhi's style of strategy is widely considered as realist one due to her strong approach in 1971 war and successful handling of the most dangerous phase of the nation when she had to confront the most powerful triangle of Pakistan, China and USA. Her daring instance comes into mind in this context when she suddenly arrived at Masco airport on the verge of 1971 war without any diplomatic formalities, that too diplomat of both India and

USSR were unaware of her Soviet visit. She called Mr. Brezhnev, the President of USSR with whom she wanted to meet on the airport. But instead of the president, Prime Minister, Mr. Kosygin, arrived to meet her at the airport with whom she refused to talk as he was a no. boss. Finally President Brezhnev himself came and succeeded to convince her and fully confirmed Soviet support in context with US nuclear threat on India. No such daring instance other than this one is available in the cotemporary world. Let us see another instance of Chinese President Mao's visit to Masco in 1953 at the time of Stalin's death. Despite staying there unusually for almost 45 days and kept on convincing new Soviet leadership to accept him being a senior most leader in the communist world as well as Chinese style of ideology, he failed to do it and finally came back empty-handed. This is the difference of leadership role between Indira Gandhi and Mao-tse-Tung. One can easily conclude the value of leadership factor in term of strategic considerations of India and China.

India's present status is the result of its own consistent efforts rather than due to any special strategic support from imperialist nation as China got from USA in terms of economic(MFN and heavy investment) and political (for membership of nuclear club and the Security Council of the UNO etc.) since 1970s. Such kind of support is in fact a very big one for a developing country. USA had given heavy economic support to Europe, Germany and Japan during post-war period but the way political support was given to China, it was unprecedented in the recent history of world. It is argued that had India got even the half of such support, it would have gone much a head of China in all aspect, although India is still not far behind China. This is the instance of main difference in strategic approach of China and India. India has committed and carried out in practice the moral value in international politics unlike China. The best way of long term strategy, according to Indian strategic culture, is to carry out ethical value and realistic base of national power together as India has been following the same uninterrupted since freedom struggle and also from the beginning of independence.

China

Unlike India-China adopts a western style of realistic strategy minus ethical element of idealism. It has been following almost all the six principles of realism propounded by Morgenthau, having its advantage and disadvantage in the contemporary strategic scenario, China looks as mostly gainer at least for a short term national interest. 'Grand strategy' of China is widely talked in the academic circle. Let me focus the same here to understand Chinese strategy based on its cultural tradition in the historical perspective.

The Peoples Republic of China (PRC) came into being in the culmination of a nearly 150 years long period of continuous turmoil and struggle against exploitation by foreign powers, domestic disruptions and factional fighting between different political forces. By the beginning of 19th century, the Qing Dynasty had already showing signs of moral decay. Historically the Chinese society has been kept together only when a strong central power ruled the county. In the Sinic system the emperor was seen as having the mandate of heaven to rule the so-called 'Middle Kingdom'. However, once he had exhausted this heavenly mandate, the people were theoretically free to search for an alternative.[10] The idea and concept of the Middle Kingdom comprising what is now east-central China, surrounded by barbarians along its vast frontiers and periphery meant that the emperor could effectively ignore the activities in the outlying area so long as these did not directly impinge on the security of the Middle Kingdom and consequently that of the emperor himself. Throughout its long history, however, China was subjected to a series of invasions mostly from the north and the northeast, which every Chinese emperor had to fight or at least resist. Some of the emperors were themselves invaders like the Mongols and Manchu. Resisting invasions, however, was a costly drain on imperial resources and usually, it was the cost of these wars that weakened the empire and made it susceptible to the next invasion.

Some of the Middle Kingdom was surrounded by 'barbarians' the Sinic hierarchical order did not recognize sovereign equality between the empire and the surrounding states or kingdom and thus only a tributary relationship existed in which the smaller states were considered inferior. In fact, until about 19th century barbarians were managing foreign affairs and interaction between people and the states was often based on Confucianism with its high ethical principles of justice, fair play and general preference of non-violent means for conflict resolution. Despite this, the Chinese did not desist from the use of military force but justified it as self-defence.[11]

The 1901 Box Rebellion staged by the local people opposed the exploitation made by foreign powers with support of the officialdom. Continuous internal disruptions and foreign interference, the Qing dynasty finally collapsed in 1911 and Dr. Sun Yat Sen established a new Republic. However, with the birth of communism in 1922, the internal turmoil stayed which led to the 40 years long civil war under Mao. After the death of Sun Yat Sen in 1927 and regime of Kuomintang Republic came into the hands of Chaing- Kai- Shek who also could not check the decaying of the regime. This nationalist regime was finally replaced by the communists under Mao in 1949. Although, the nationalist was defeated but not eliminated as they fled to Formosa (Taiwan) just across the Taiwan Strait and continued armed attack against mainland-PRC with US backing. The PRC leadership, it looks, develop a xenophobia, and remained a paranoid power ever since.[12]

In course of building up, reorganization and

reconstruction of internal and external resources, PRC concentrated on various fronts. Keeping in view American supporting Taiwan and the threat of war looming large on the Korean peninsula, Mao's first major strategic move was to find a dependable friend. He tried to build a strategic and ideologically strengthen relations with Soviet Union and he succeeded to do it without much effort in view of cold war between the two super powers. USSR, with the signing of the 'Treaty of Friendship' on 14 Feb 1950, provided China all the possible economic, technological, industrial, financial, military hardware and various other assistance required for developing an underdeveloped country.

In 1937, even 12 years before his regime was resumed in 1949, Mao had planned to incorporate Tibet, the Buddhist dominated region and Xinjiang, the Muslim majority as autonomous provinces of the PRC. Immediately after taking over the charge of PRC in 1950 he sent the PLA to 'liberate' Xinjiang and Tibet 'from the oppression of feudal orthodox and blind faith'. Both the provinces had been historically the home of anti-Chinese revolt and never accepted Chinese sovereignty. He intended to consolidate/ensure border security by incorporating Tibet against newly independent democratic India, and Xinjiang against the world leader of communism, Russia, despite the fact that there was no sign of threat at all either from Delhi or Masco at that point of time. This is an instance of Mao's style of strategy of realism based on the old saying of 'no one is permanent friend or enemy in international politics'.

Taking into account the US support to Taiwan, Japan and its involvement on Korean issue, PRC joined Korean conflict with Soviet support to protect it from American intention of imposing imperialism in the region and China as well. By the end of 1950s China started giving indications of a possible conflict against India and the USSR in the near future on the pretext of imaginary border issue with India and the supply of a small nuclear bomb and ideological issue after the death of Stalin with Soviet Union. The war designed strategy of Mao came true in 1962 against India and in 1965 against USSR when PLA directly confronted against Indian and Soviet forces respectively. Being a true follower of Morgenthau, Mao believed in the promotion of national interest at any cost – even at the cost of India and Soviet Union, the most reliable friend in the region and the world as well. This strategy was a well thought planning in advance to shake hands with USA in the near future. PRC had already enjoyed all the possible maximum support from India (on Tibet and recognition of PRC) and the USSR (building up PLA, technology etc), now Mao wanted to focus on USA for political (for UNO) and economic support irrespective of ideological issue – capitalism vs. communism. And he achieved this goal in 1970 with Nixon – Kissinger regime of USA. Not the end of strategic aspiration here, China now dreams of pushing USA behind existing global status.

Chinese strategy towards India and the strategic rivalry between the two in the given situation are focused below:

1. Golden Period from 1949 to 1958

The policy of 'China and India as brothers' (Hindi-Chini bhai-bhai) followed between 1949 to 1958. During this period India, being the second non –communist country after Burma, recognized PRC against the desire of entire western powers. Besides, Prime Ministers of both the countries visited each other and agreed to follow the policy of Panchsheel. Moreover, India accepted Tibet as part of Chinese sovereignty during this time. And they also attended Bandung conference together during this period. That is why this period is known as golden period in the modern history of China and India.

2. Chinese Policy of Containment from 1959 to 1978

China raised border issue during this phase of

relationship. This new face of China was not at all a surprise move. Border demarcation issue was taken up between British-India and Sun-Yat-Sen regime of China in Shimla in 1914. Both accepted Mc Mohn Line in principle only, not in practice. Communist party of China opposed it from the very beginning of its foundation in 1922. The same party came into power in 1949 in the name of PRC and it raised this issue subsequently in a tactical move after 1956, by that time China had already taken all possible support from India during the aforesaid previous phase. However, in view of the above, it cannot be said that PRC's policy of raising border issue at this stage was the new one or it was a surprise move. Before India could prepare her military muscle, China attacked India in Oct. 1962. It resulted into the beginning of dark period almost for two decades in the history of centuries old relationship between the two great civilizations. After 1962 war Sino-India relations were cold and hostile. In John Garver's view, this hostility reflected an underlying geopolitical rivalry between the two, both nations seeking to restore their traditional great-power status and with overlapping traditional spheres of influence. Garver sees rivalry and mutual perceptions of military threat as constant features of Sino-Indian relations.[13] China made all possible strategic efforts during this period to contain India and prevent it from dominating the subcontinent including its support to Pakistan during 1965 war and also supported Pakistan policy on Kashmir.

3. Strategy of Rapprochement from 1979 to 1997

In 1976 Mao Zedong died, and in 1979 Deng Xiaoping initiated an ambitious new policy of economic reform. Deng recognized that to concentrate on economic modernization, China needed a peaceful and stable environment, which in turn would require a reorientation of China's foreign policies. For the first time in Chinese modern history, the country developed a coherent, integrated Asia regional policy, consisting of pragmatic relations with the two superpowers and improved ties with all the countries on its periphery.[14] In 1979 and 1981, the Chinese and Indian foreign ministers exchanged visits, though during Indian foreign minister, Atal Behari Bajpayee's Feb. 1979 visit, he was embarrassed by Chinese poorly timed or deliberately done invasion of Vietnam. However, he succeeded to bring home Chinese commitment to cease support for insurgency in northeast region of India. Between 1981 and 1987 China and India held eight rounds of negotiations on their boundary but failed to produce a solution. Yet during 1988 visit of Indian PM, Rajeev Gandhi, Deng told him "Let both sides forget the unpleasant period in our past relations, and let us treat everything with an eye on the future."[15] During Narsimha Rao's visit to China in 1093, both the countries signed the agreement on the 'Maintenance of Peace and Tranquility along the line of actual control.' Moreover, in 1996 Chinese president Jiang Zemin visited New Delhi and signed yet another agreement- 'Confidence Building Measures' in the military field and along the LAC' to solidify the relationship between the two. In its most significant gesture to promote rapprochement during this period, China, shifting from her earlier approach, unilaterally declared that Kashmir is a bilateral issue between India and Pakistan and hence both should resolve it peacefully.

4. Strategic Setting in 1998

Chinese senior General Fu Quanyou's Visit to India from 27-30 April 1998, first by a PLA chief of general staff, was scheduled, Mr. George Fernandes, then defence minister of India, publicly alleged, ten days before General's visit, that China was continuing to carry out border incursions. Even during visit of the General, Fernandes once again lambasted China publicly, accusing it of being the number one threat to Indian security, even greater than Pakistan. The May 11 and 13, 1998 Indian nuclear test followed, occurring even before General returned Beijing on May 18, 1998. Was the timing of nuclear test deliberately scheduled to humiliate China to pay back the Chinese for embarrassment they had caused then foreign minister Vajpayee when they had attacked Vietnam, a friendly country of India, during his 1979 visit to China, forcing him to cut his trip short? This is a matter of speculation. The Chinese official response to Indian nuclear test was reflected in People's Daily on 15 May 1998 that "The Indian govt. has disregarded the fundamental interest of the vast number of its people and desperately developed nuclear weapon in defiance of world opinion. The reason for this is nothing less than a desire to threaten neighboring countries and dominate South Asia."[16] On 13 May, The New York Times published a letter from PM Vajpayee to president Bill Clinton, leaked in the USA, which blamed China for India's nuclear test, saying that "I have been deeply concerned at the deteriorating security environment, especially the nuclear environment, faced by India for some years past. We have an overt nuclear weapon state on our borders, a state which committed armed aggression against India in 1962. Although our relations with that country improved in the last decade or so, an atmosphere of distrust persists mainly due to the unresolved border problem. To add to the distrust that country has materially helped another neighbor of ours to become a covert nuclear weapon state. At the hands of this bitter neighbor we have suffered three aggressions in the last 50 years."[17] In reaction to this letter, the 19 May People's Daily further condemned Indian nuclear test more strongly, that "...nobody believe such preposterous logic and the so called 'China threat' lies.[18] However, immediately after India, Pakistan's test for nuclear weapon on 28 and 30 May 1998, might cautioned Chinese President for toning down the tamper, who subsequently said "...no matter whether India or Pakistan, conducting nuclear test, is against world trend," and he urged both countries to "keep calm, show restraint, and reopen dialogue," and to sign unconditionally NPT and CTBT.[19]

5. Strategy of Engagement

Anyway, only a few months after the nuclear test, China resumed its efforts to engage India diplomatically both on political and Joint Working Group level. Initial setback and bettering due to nuclear test could not stop China and India to normalize relations and to proceed ahead. During Vajpayee's visit (being the PM) to China in June 2003 both sides finally agreed for further discussions on border delimitation. The most important thing had happened at this occasion was Chinese recognition to Sikkim as part of India and to reopen trade route through Chumbi Vally. Both the countries are developing in a remarkable phase of bilateral relationship in the area of economic, trade, information technology etc. for the first time in last 66 years.

Their mutual trade and commerce has almost touched 70 billion dollars - India's highest bilateral trade with any one country - and they are targeting at 100 billion dollars by 2020.A part from it, their understanding and co-operation in the World Trade Organization is also a matter of appreciation.

6. Strategic Encirclement

However, it is argued that China's hostile acts as well as friendly gesture, both are unpredictable, unreliable and mysterious. India is well experienced of Chinese such behavior in the past. It is said that China, unfortunately, understands only the language of muscles power, nothing else. Despite a very close economic tie with India, it is reluctant to settle border issue, the root cause of all the problems, even after consistent efforts at the level of JWG and political leadership since 1980. Besides, military modernization, unlawful demand of access to sea and land towards China Sea and Island of Japan etc., continuous incursions on LOC with India, encircling India from all directions by gaining strategic access to Maldives, Sri Lanka, Myanmar, Bangladesh, Nepal, Pakistan, Southeast Asia, Asia Pacific, Central Asia and

Middle East etc. speak the truth. Knowing intentions of China, India is getting prepared accordingly. Now one thing appears to clear that China cannot afford to take India for granted as it did in 1962.

7. Strategic Triangles

The concept of a strategic triangle has become familiar to analysts of international affairs. It refers to a situation in which three major powers are sufficiently important to each other that a change in the relationship between any two of them has a significant impact on the interest of the third. The greater that impact, actual or potential, the greater is the significant of the triangular relationship.[20] The most familiar strategic triangles in the contemporary era have been Sino-Soviet- American during the cold war and now China –India-America. Although, Harry Harding also includes Sino-Japan-America during the cold war period in the list of strategic triangle, but many other scholars argues that all the three partners in this case do not have equal elements for being a global power or at least the capability of growing as world power in future. Japan in particular appears to be weak element due to its dependence for her security on USA under Japan-US treaty of 1953. As regards Sino-Indian-American triangle is concerned, its features are appended as under:

1. These three partners have formed triangle ever since India got independence, China became communist and USA became a permanent player in Asia.
2. India despite gaining all essential elements of a world power, it is taken as a weaker partner, hence both China and USA attempt to use India to contain each other. In view of standing in the centre, India is taking advantage from both of them. Indo-US Civil Nuclear Deal of 2008 and having a highest trade relation with China in the world are obviously the instances of India's strategic advantage of being a partner of this triangle.

3. Although, India is also in the triangle like group comprising Sino-Russia-India that is called as nexus. But it cannot be conceptualized as triangle like that of Sino-India-America, because Russia is no longer an active player in Asia. However, Russian position in this case of nexus is strategically better due to its military arms and equipments required for both India and China and in this situation Russians are gainer in term of bargaining with both of them on its supply.

Assessment

In view of the above the assessment in nutshell are as under:

a. Both China and India are growing as active players in the multi-polar global strategic scenario in future.

b. Whether China likes or not, India is presently a joint regional power in Asia along with China. Japan is not in the race due to its dependence on USA for national security.

c. Both China and India produce such a heavy share of global GDP that rest of the world cannot afford to ignore them particularly in the WTO.

d. Chinese use of Pakistan to contain India has not produced any sustentative strategic gain for China, despite Chinese unlawful supply of missiles and nuclear material to it for which China has been condemned worldwide. Sooner or later, China would prefer to alter this policy in view of growing Indian strategic statures as well as growing terror act in China for which Indian co-operation would be required for joint strategy against terrorism.

e. Unsettled border dispute is a long term part of Chinese strategy against India. It serves two vital Chinese strategic interests – 1. India's limited resources are diverted to defence budget for keeping a big army for caring a long boundary and 2. The development suffers due to this unproductive expenditure. It helps China as it prevents India to counter China in term of economic growth. Hence China would prefer unsettled border in future too. To counter such Chinese strategy India is taking Japan and other countries of Asia Pacific and South East Asia with its side and encircles China, so as to keep it under limit.

f. India is fully aware that both China and USA are most unreliable and hence as far as possible it would take advantage of being a partner of the strategic triangle and in the meanwhile it would strengthen her status.

g. Strategic pressure on China from all sides in the region and India/ USA as well, might force it to collapse like USSR.

Conclusion

Prime Minister Jawahar Lal Nehu said in Lok Sabha on Nov. 25, 1959 that "From fairly early in history, they (China) have had a sensation of greatness. They call themselves the 'Middle Kingdom', and it seemed natural to them that other countries should pay tribute to them. Their thinking was that the rest of the world occupied a lower grade. That has made it difficult for us to understand the working of their mind, and what is more to the point, for them to understand the working of our mind."[21] This statement of Pt. Nehru is still relevant even after four decades. His statement is a suitable conclusion of Indo-China strategic rivalry.

References

1. Phadke Ramesh, China's Power Projection (New Delhi: Manas Publication, 2005), p.186.

2. John Glenn and Stuart Poore, Neorealism vs. Strategic Culture, p. 47

3. Colin S. Gray, Strategy and History: Essays on Theory and Practice, p. 162

4. Menon Nárayan, "India –China Border Issues: Strategic Implications and Impact of Air Power", paper presented in a seminar organized by YCNISDA, University of Pune.
5. Indian Strategic Culture, The Washington Quarterly, Winter 1992, P. 129.
6. Ibid, p. 130.
7. Stephen P. Cohen, India: Emerging Power, Washington CD, Brookings Institution Press, 2001, p.126.
8. Susan L. Shirk, One side Rivalry: China's Perceptions and Policies toward India, The India – China Relationship, Rivalry and Engagement, Oxford University Press, 2004, p. 75.
9. Phadke Ramesh, p. 141
10. Phadke Ramesh, p. 19-21.
11. Ibid.
12. Ibid., p. 22
13 Susan L.Shirk, P. 77
14 Ibid., p.80
15. Ibid, p.81
16. Ibid, p. 86
17. Ibid., p. 83
18. Ibid.,p. 87
19. Ibid., p.84
20. Harding Harry, The Evolution Of The Strategic Triangle: China, India And The United States, The India –China Relationship: Rivalry And Engagement (Oxford University Press, 2001), p. 321.
21. Menon Narayan, "India-China Border Issues Strategic Implications and Impact of Air Power", Paper presented in YC-NISDA, University of Pune.

8

Sino-Indian Relations in the context of South Asia : (Pakistan as a factor)

Dr. K.S. Sidhu

India and China are world's oldest civilizations and have co-existed in peace for millennia. Both countries have effectively tried to reignite cultural, diplomatic and economic ties. Both are world's most populous countries and fastest growing major economics. The far-reaching growth in China and India's global diplomatic and economic influence has also enhanced the significance of their bilateral relationship and, more particularly, in the South Asian context. China has emerged as the largest trading partner of India and two countries have tried to expand their strategic and military relations.

Beijing's South Asia policy is tied to China's military security concerns vis-a-vis that of India and territorial disputes. Chinese leaders regularly visit Nepal, Bangladesh

---

Professor in Defence Studies (Retd.), *Kssidhu40@hotmail.com* and Sri Lanka to demonstrate a continuing determination to remain involved in South Asia and to reassure China's friends that improvement in Sino–Indian relations would not be at their cost.

However, Pakistan has occupied a prominent place in the geo-strategic milieu with regard to the South Asian region. Beijing's entente cordiale with Pakistan continues to flourish, prominently underpinned by nuclear and missile co-operation. India continues to keep a close eye on the political and strategic relations between China and India's neighbours. Current strategic and economic trends indicate that South Asia's importance in China's national security calculus is likely to increase in the 21st century.

India and China have some striking similarities. Both are ancient civilizations, reincarnated as modern republics in the mid twentieth century, and are now rising powers. Both have nuclear weapons, burgeoning economies, expanding military budgets and large reservoirs of manpower, and seem to be vying for influence in the Indian Ocean, the Persian Gulf, Africa, Central Asia and East Asia. The Sino-Indian relationship is more often seen in terms of the countries' interactions with India, Pakistan and other South Asian nations. It is also defined by contrasting polities and models of development, with the parties silently competing for capital, resources and markets.

Since the first century A.D, with the spread of Buddhism from India to China, both the nations had wide ranging cultural contact. However, they had conflict of interests in Tibet. At the end of its civil war in 1949, China wanted to reassert control over Tibet and to set free the Tibetan people from Lamaism and Feudalism by the use of arms in 1950. Nehru communicated Chinese leaders that India had not any political, territorial interests or to seek special principles in Tibet. With Indian support, Tibetan delegates signed an agreement in May 1951 recognizing

Chinese sovereignty assuming that the existing political and social system in Tibet would carry on. In 1954, India China signed an eight years agreement in Tibet that lay out the foundation of their relationship in the form of *Panchasheela*. The slogan in 1950s was *'Hindi-Chini-Bhai-Bhai'*.

South Asia ranks third in importance after the Northeast and Southeast Asian regions in China's Asia policy. China shares common borders with four (Bhutan, India, Nepal and Pakistan) out of seven South Asian states (the other three are Bangladesh, Sri Lanka and the Maldives), making it an integral part of South Asia. China's military security concerns *vis-a-vis* South Asia's largest and most powerful state, India, coupled with territorial disputes and the need to protect its 'soft strategic underbelly', i.e. Tibet, provide a key tounderstanding Beijing's South Asia policy.[1]

The boundary disputesamong South Asian have shaped China's relations with South Asia. Whilst Beijing has resolved its disputed boundaries with Nepal and Pakistan, territorial disputes with India and Bhutan are yet to be resolved. Much like China, the states of South Asia are multi-ethnic, multi-religious, multi-lingual and multi-cultural. All South Asian states have historic, cultural, linguistic, and religious ethnic links with India and they all share borders with India rather than with each other. The postcolonial geopolitical landscape has created a number of overlapping ethno-religious and linguistic problems in South Asia. For example, Bengalis live in Bangladesh as well as in India; Kashmiris, Sindhis and Punjabis live in both India and Pakistan; more Tamils live in India than in Sri Lanka; Nepalese live in Nepal as well in India and Bhutan; and Tibetans live in China as well as in India, Nepal and Bhutan. Internal security issues in one state inevitably have external security ramifications.

China's relations with India, during the last decade,

have gone through a roller coaster from the highs of the early and mid 1990s to the lows of the late 1990s. Sino–Indian relations remain poor, with or without a risk of confrontation, despite a dramatic increase in bilateral exchanges at the political, economic, military, andcultural levels including some high-level visits. Beijing's entente cordiale[2] with Pakistan continues to flourish, underpinned by nuclear and missile co-operation. Chinese leaders regularly visit Nepal, Bangladesh and Sri Lanka to demonstrate a continuing determination to remain involved in South Asia and a desire to reassure China's friends in the region thatimprovement in Sino–Indian relations would not be at their cost. New Delhi keeps a closeeye on the political and strategic relations between China and India's neighbours.

Main Features of China's South Asia Policy

A prominent feature of Beijing's South Asia policy has been its 'India-centric' approach, which, in turn, has seen military links with India's neighbours dominating the policy agenda. The major objective of China's Asia policy has been to prevent the rise of a peer competitor, a real Asian rival to challenge China's status as the Asia–Pacific's sole 'Middle Kingdom'. Beijing has always known that India, if it ever gets its economic and strategic acts together, alone hasthe size, might, numbers and, above all, the intention to match China. In the meantime, perceiving India as weak, in decisive and on the verge of collapse, Beijing took the view thatall that was needed was to keep New Delhi under pressure by arming its neighbours and supporting insurgency movements in India's minority regions. All of India's neighbours have obtained much of their military arsenal from China—indeed 90 per cent of China's arms sales go to countries that border India. For its part, Beijing has justified military relations between itself and South Asian countries as legitimate and normal state-to-state relations well within the purview of the Five Principles of

Peaceful Coexistence.[3]

Broadly speaking, India's relations with South Asian states have been guided by two major concerns: (1) geostrategic concerns, that is, a desire to insulate the Subcontinent from adverse external forces that might 'fish in troubled waters' and thus destabilize India's security environment; and (2) geopolitical concerns, that is, a desire to ensure that geographical proximity and ethno-religious affinities do not lead to instability on or near its borders, particularly as they inevitably affect India's domestic, ethnic, religious and political relationships, and could give rise to secessionist demands within India. India has since independence resorted to a combination of diplomatic, economic and military means to establish cordial atmosphere in South Asia. For instance, in 1949–1950, India signed treaties with Bhutan, Nepal and the small protectorate of Sikkim to strengthen its close links with the Himalayan kingdoms, and it took on the responsibility of securing their northern frontiers with China. However, South Asian states have always resented India's hegemonic ambitions in the region and have tried to resist the imposition of the Indian version of the Monroe Doctrine by seeking to build security links with extra-regional powers, mainly China and the United States, as a counterweight to India's domineering role. This has led to ongoing conflict between South Asia's largest state and its smaller neighbours.

Beijing's perspective, 'whether China and Nepal, Sri Lanka, Bangladesh, or Pakistan wish any particular relations is exclusively for them to decide. For India to attempt to dictate or limit those relations is unacceptable.' In their meetings with these countries, the Chinese continue to bemoan India's 'big brotherly' and 'hegemonic attitude'. Emphasising that 'all countries, big or small, should be treated equally', Beijing has long been critical of the useof coercive strategies aimed at ensuring New Delhi's security interests are not compromised by their ties with China.[4] Because of the asymmetry in size and might, India is invariably drawn into the big-brother syndrome or 'small state versus big state syndrome' in relation to its smaller neighbours. Whenever South Asian countries have tried to play 'the China card' in their relations with India, problems have arisen between India and China as well as between India and its South Asian neighbours.

Further, China remains a major economic aid donor to Bangladesh, Nepal, Pakistan and Sri Lanka. China's use of economic means in its rivalry with India for influence in Nepal and Bangladesh is a case in point. Beijing's economic ties with South Asian states supplement and reinforce its military security objectives and goals. Despite some improvement in Sino–Indian ties since the early 1990s, Beijing has not lost its motivations to prop up these smaller states against India. However, in contrast with Southeast and Northeast Asia, the interplay between economics and security is rather weak in South Asia, since geostrategic considerations predominantly shape China's policy towards the region. Beijing's rhetoric aboutthe Five Principles of Peaceful Coexistence notwithstanding, classic Chinese statecraft dictates that there is no such thing as friendly foreign powers: 'All states are either hostileor subordinate'.[5]

Subordinate states areallies/dependents which need to be protected and provided with economic and military support whereas hostile states are enemies which need to be subdued by involving them in trouble some embroilments. Recognising India as one of its major strategic rivals, China has since 1963 firmly aligned itself with Pakistan to contain the common enemy. Critics argue that Beijing's policy towards the sub-continental rivals has been based on the classic strategic principle of 'make the barbarians fight while you watch from the mountain top'.[6]

Despite Chinese efforts to justify military links with

Pakistan as part of 'normal state-to-state relations', India has remained unconvinced, seeing them as 'hostile' and 'threatening' in both intent and character so asto tie India down south of the Himalayas. The 1990s saw the issue of Beijing's nuclear and missile assistance to Pakistan overshadow the thorny territorial dispute between India and China. For India, Pakistan is not and cannot be a threat without China's military support. Independent India since Nehru's days has entertained hopes of joint Sino–Indian leadership of Asia to counter Western influence, but the Chinese have shown no enthusiasm for sharing leadership of Asia with anyone, least of all India. From New Delhi's perspective, Beijing's gradual but subtle penetration deep into southern Asia in the second half of the 20th century has been primarily at India's expense. Here it is worth recalling that, historically and civilisationally, India, as the pivotal power in South Asia, perceives itself much as China has traditionally perceived itself in relation to East Asia.

India's strategic analysts have always emphasised the need to keep up militarily with China. India's defence policy has long been based on the principle of 'keeping onestep ahead of Pakistan and at par with China'. Initially, India's nuclear capability was aimed solely at deterring China, not Pakistan. It is the adversarial nature of the Sino–Indian relationship which has driven India's and, in turn, Pakistan's nuclear weapons program. The strategic space in which India traditionally operated had become increasingly constricted due to Chinese penetration, became further evident from Beijing's forays into Burma and the Bay of Bengal in the 1990s.[7]

The 1998 Indian nuclear tests were preceded by the then Indian Defence Minister statements calling China a 'bigger potential threat' than Pakistan and describing how his country was being 'encircled' by Chinese military activities in Tibet and military alliances with Pakistan and Burma.

Chinese analysts have accused India, particularly since India's nuclear tests in May 1998,of pursuing a policy of military expansion since attaining independence, in order to become a global military power, contain China, and dominate and control South Asia and the Indian Ocean. While major Western powers have, however grudgingly, accepted the reality of India's nuclear capability, there is no sign of Beijing softening its demand that New Delhi initiate a complete rollback of its nuclear weapons program and unconditionally sign the Comprehensive Test Ban Treaty (CTBT) and the Nuclear Non-Proliferation Treaty (NPT)as per UN Security Council resolution 1172.[8]

Despite the existence of some asymmetry: China is a more fraught subject in Indian national debates than India is for China. China does not appear to feel threatened in any serious way by India, while India at times displays tremendous insecurity in the face of Chinese economic success and military expansion. Not much has changed in the rhetoric of Sino-Indian relations since Mao Zedong, speaking in 1951 in honour of the first anniversary of India's constitution, declared that 'excellent friendship' had existed between the two countries 'for thousands of years'.[9]

The modern Sino-Indian relationship has been marked by four distinct phases. Purported friendship and ideological congruence around anti-imperialist foreign-policy objectives from 1950 deteriorated into a bitter yet brief border conflict in 1962, followed by a Sino-Indian 'Cold War'.[10] In 1998, India pointed to China as the justification for its second round of nuclear tests (the first had occurredin 1974). Although this might have been expected to create significant tensions between the two nations, economic relations have since intensified. Nonetheless, the period from 1998 onward remains one of uncertainty and occasional antagonism, marked by China's full emergence as a global power and the courting of India by other powers, not least the United States, as an important nation not just in its own right but also as a potential counterweight to Chinese power and regional influence.[11]

One important wild card could be domestic sub-nationalism, which afflicts both China and India, but with different characteristics and consequences. India has survived as a nation by cobbling together a sometimes conciliatory and often weak political and security response to various insurgencies and separatist movements. China, on the other hand, still very much relies on the heavy hand of the state to suppress such uprisings, as seen in Tibet in 2008 and Xinjiang in 2009. Ethnic unrest in China's peripheral territories – Xinjiang, Tibet, Taiwan, Manchuria, Mongolia – has historically been a major vulnerability for the Chinese state, as such episodes could possibly invite foreign involvement.[12]

On land, the ring of states that the British once used as buffers for the Raj—Bhutan, Nepal, Afghanistan, and Myanmar—has fallen under increasing Chinese influence, with Beijing buoyed by the fastest-growing major economy in the world and a willingness to cut deals with regimes of all stripes. Even when India held a 30 percent stake in Myanmar's Shwe gas field, Myanmar's junta chose to sell gas from that field to China instead. In Nepal, where Indian security agencies long held sway and often dictated the political process, the ascendance of Maoists along with Chinese reconstruction activities shattered the illusion that the country was, like the Himalayas, a bulwark for the subcontinent.

China's Primary Strategic Objectives

The primary objectives of the Chinese Policy are to maintain an external environment conducive to the pursuit of economic reform, expand its strategic independence and leverage in a multi-polar environment, and continue strengthening itself. The Chinese view is slowly turning to accommodate the facts that India is already a dominant power in South Asia and is rapidly becoming a major world player. Therefore, India has to be engaged in a positive manner, even if it is at some cost to China's relationship with Pakistan. Major contentious bilateral issues like the border problem and China's support to Pakistan presently continue to evade mutually acceptable solutions. However, pragmatic policy analysts believe that despite divergent security perceptions, both countries can seize the opportunity to forge mutually beneficial bilateral trade and more importantly, a durable strategic partnership.

China has been redefining its national identity and has been reconstructing its strategic culture. Chinese diplomacy has undergone an important evolution over the last decade. Beijing's foreign policy reflects a more confident, less confrontational and more proactive approach towards regional and global affairs. These trends are reflected in China's increased engagement with multilateral and regional security organizations and Beijing's growing attention to non-traditional security challenges. By following a cooperative policy, China is showing that it is now a stabilizing rather than a destabilising factor.

China's Strategic Objectives and Threat Perceptions

China's desire to gain "great power" status on the world stage is reflected in its greater economic leverage over countries in the region and elsewhere, as well as its steps to strengthen its military. East Asian states are adapting to the advent of a more powerful China by forging closer economic and political ties with Beijing, potentially accommodating themselves to its preferences, particularly on sensitive issues like Taiwan. China is continuing to strengthen its military through developing and acquiring modern weapons, including advanced fighter aircraft, sophisticated submarines and increasing numbers of ballistic missiles. China will overtake Russia and others as the second largest defence spender after the United States over the next two decades and will be, by any measure, a first-rate military power. If China's economy takes a downward turn, regional security would weaken, resulting in heightened prospects for political instability, crime, narcotics trafficking, and illegal migration.

Like China, India is also becoming an economic magnet for the region, and its rise is impacting not only South Asia but also the North, Central and West Asia, and other countries of Southeast Asia. India seeks to bolster regional cooperation both for strategic reasons and because of its desire to increase its leverage with the West, including in such organizations as the WTO. As India's economy grows governments in Southeast Asia, that is, Malaysia, Singapore, Thailand, and others would move closer to India to help build a potential geopolitical counterweight to China. At the same time, India seeks to strengthen its ties with countries in the region without excluding China.

China seeks to acquire and establish a favourable security environment that is conducive to continued economic growth and its military modernization. However, the key notion behind China's overall national objectives can be found in its "Comprehensive National Power" concept, which asserts that military modernization is the key in protecting China's security and unity, as well as building a prosperous society. In short, China's primary strategic objectives in the international arena are driven by the following requirements:[13]

(a) Maintaining an external environment conducive to the pursuit of economic reform, opening to the outside world, and economic construction.

(b) Preserving or expanding China's strategic independence and leverage in a complex multi-polar environment.

(c) Furthering its efforts to reunify Taiwan with the nation.

(d) Strengthening its ability to defend against external

pressures or attacks, emerging from highly complex and uncertain, yet arguably less immediately threatening security environment.

There are three major tasks of historic significance for China: to propel the modernization drive; to achieve national reunification; and to safeguard world peace and promote common development.[14] To accomplish these tasks, China has developed some new concepts for its national strategy:

First, it seeks to work with the international community to maintain regional stability. China will continue to improve and cultivate relations with both developing and developed countries. Proceeding from the fundamental interests of all countries concerned, China will broaden the converging points of common interests and properly settle differences on the basis of the Five Principles of Peaceful Co-existence, notwithstanding the differences in social systems and ideologies. China will increasingly cooperate with the United States and other countries in dealing with regional security problems.

Second, it stresses new concepts of security, primarily mutual trust, mutual benefit, equality, and coordination. Since the end of the Cold War, China has changed its security concepts according to the evolving international situation and interests of the Chinese people as well as the necessity for world peace and development. China believes that to obtain lasting peace, it is imperative to abandon the Cold War mentality, cultivate a new concept of security, and seek new ways to safeguard peace. It has to be kept in mind that the new concepts of security are in keeping with the trend of the era and have greater relevance. China holds that the core of this new security concept should be mutual trust, mutual benefit, equality, and coordination.[15]

The new security concept should be the guideline to resolve regional disputes as well as improve international security.[16] Third, China seeks to resolve the disputes in the South China Sea and improve its relations with neighboring countries. China's existing guideline is to advance development, peace, and stability in Asia. It is an important part of China's development strategy to maintain good relationships with its neighbors, make them secure, and help them prosper.[17]

Sharing a common border with China of around 7,000 kilometers, Southern Asia is critical to Beijing's interests. In terms of security, this region is particularly significant to the stability of China's three frontier provinces, Tibet, Xinjiang, and Yunnan, especially after the violent riots in Tibet in March 2008 and in Xinjiang in July 2009. Tibet is a significant security concern. Indian parliamentarian and author Arun Shourie argues that 'India's security is inextricably intertwined with the existence and survival of Tibet as a buffer state and to the survival and strengthening of Tibetan culture and religion'.[18]

With about 120,000 exiled Tibetans living in India and Nepal (including the Dalai Lama and the so-called Tibetan Government in Exile in India) and some Uighur militants based in the tribal areas of Afghanistan and Pakistan, the willingness and capability of these countries to cooperate are critical to China's efforts to counter secessionism in Tibet and Xinjiang. In 2008, the Indian government took great pains to ensure that Tibetan protestors did not cause any embarrassment to Beijing during the passage of the Olympic Torch through New Delhi.[19]

The greatest threat to the Indo-Chinese relationship arises from widely differing views of the history and ultimate destiny of Tibet. For China, India's recognition of Tibet as part of China seems grudging and conditional. And its role as host of the Dalai Lama and his 'splittist clique', to use Beijing's colourful phrase, could appear to some Chinese as a threat to their country's cohesion. For India, Chinese repression in Tibet is painful, and many Indians hope it will ultimately prove futile. Careful management by both capitals will be required to prevent developments relating to Tibet from undermining the wider China–India relationship.

Economically speaking, Southern Asia has a significant bearing on the development of China's western region, Chinese enterprises' "go global" strategy, and China's energy security. The subcontinent is a gateway to the Indian Ocean for China's western region. Southern Asia is already a major destination of China's overseas projects contracting, and with nearly a quarter of the world's population, the region holds great potential as a market for China's commodities and investments. With its geographical advantage in the Indian Ocean, the subcontinent plays an important role in safeguarding the sea lines of communication, on which China's energy importing and foreign trade are heavily dependent. Politically speaking, China views countries in Southern Asia as important partners in restructuring the regional and global institutions and fending off Western pressure on such issues as human rights and climate change. Countries in the region are committed to the one-China policy and have firmly supported China on the issue of Taiwan.

Against the backdrop of these multifaceted interests, China's strategic objectives in the region are to reinforce a friendly Southern Asia that is willing to extend support for China's efforts to safeguard its national unity and integrity; to promote a stable Southern Asia that is capable of ensuring the safety of Chinese citizens and investments in the region; and to build a prosperous Southern Asia that is likely to create more opportunities for China's sustainable development. Together, these objectives serve the fundamental task of China's foreign policy that is, "securing a long-term and favorable external environment for China's development."

Since the end of the Cold War and the normalization

of Sino-Indian relations, China has not perceived any serious strategic threats from Southern Asia. Indirect threats, however, abound. One that China is monitoring is the Indo-Pakistani rivalry. Because China shares borders with both India and Pakistan, any conflict between the two nuclear powers would force China to take sides and also have direct implications for the security of China's western frontier region. China is also keeping tabs on drug trafficking that originates in Afghanistan and Myanmar. Because of instability and poor governance in those countries, drug trafficking and organized crime have increasingly threatened to spill over into Xinjiang and Yunnan.

China and the South Asian States

The U.S. led war on terror in Afghanistan has forced China to look southwest. After China started its economic reforms in 1978, it gradually strengthened its ties with South Asia in general, and neighboring countries now are given "first priority" over major powers in China's foreign policy. China has officially outlined four pillars in its foreign policy platform: major powers are the key, surrounding areas are the first priority, developing countries are the foundation, and multilateral forums are the important stage.

China has also improved its relations with the rising global power India, long viewed as hostile, going back to the 1962 border war, but now acknowledged to be rising into a global power. And China's strategy on the large-scale development of its western region has triggered the enthusiasm of local governments in Xinjiang, Tibet, and Yunnan to establish closer economic links with South Asia.

Thanks to the globalized economy of China and its heavy dependence on Middle East oil, the significance of the smaller South Asian countries—Nepal, Bhutan, Bangladesh, Sri Lanka, and Maldives—have dramatically increased. Bangladesh and Sri Lanka have become two of the major destinations for China's overseas contracted projects and investments, while, because of their specific geographical locations, Sri Lanka, Maldives, and Bangladesh are relevant to China's energy security. With nearly 200,000 Chinese tourists visiting Maldives each year, Beijing can no longer neglect the small island country in the Indian Ocean.The fact that the subcontinent is part of China's neighborhood as well is usually overlooked, while some strategic elites in India construe China's closer links with the smaller countries as China's encirclement of India, the so-called string of pearls strategy. Despite sharing borders with six South Asian countries, the People's Republic of China has long attached insufficient importance to South Asia. Since entering the new century, however, the significance of Southern Asia to China has been upgraded and the Chinese government is paying more attention to its relationship with the region. After China started its economic reforms in 1978, it gradually strengthened its ties with South Asia in general, and neighboring countries now are given "first priority" over major powers in China's foreign policy. China has also improved its relations with the rising global power India, long viewed as hostile, going back to the 1962 border war, but now acknowledged to be rising into a global power. And China's strategy on the large-scale development of its western region has triggered the enthusiasm of local governments in Xinjiang, Tibet, and Yunnan to establish closer economic links with South Asia.

Afghanistan adds a layer of complexity to relations in Southern Asia. Besides being relevant to China's Xinjiang region in terms of countering secessionism and counter-narcotics efforts, Afghanistan's stability is directly related to the stability of Pakistan, another important neighbor of China in the region. Therefore, China expects an independent, stable, and friendly Afghanistan. The latest China-Afghanistan strategic partnership indicates China's long-term commitment to Afghan reconstruction and reconciliation. As for India's role in Afghanistan, China views its development assistance as impressive and positive. Its only concern is about an ongoing rivalry between India and Pakistan mainly on the Kashmir issue and their confrontation in Afghanistan. Many Chinese scholars believe that unless this rivalry is eased, Pakistan will continue to see Afghanistan as a vital strategic bulwark against India, while India views Afghanistan as another strategic front against Pakistan. If India tries to create an anti-Pakistan Afghanistan and Pakistan tries to create an anti-India Afghanistan, reconciliation in Afghanistan would be far harder to achieve.

Myanmar, which shares a border of nearly 2,200 kilometers with China, has a great deal of strategic significance for China. Beyond the stability of the border areas that are affected by drug trafficking and ethnic insurgency in Myanmar, China is concerned about the security of its enormous investments in Myanmar's infrastructure and power plants. The country's geographical location also provides China shorter and more convenient access to the Indian Ocean, which well serves both the development of the poor economies in southwestern China and China's energy security by providing an alternate route for energy supplies to travel. It is against this backdrop that China is building an oil and gas pipeline across Myanmar into southwestern China. Standard realist accounts argue China is unwilling to permit the emergence of India as a power beyond South Asia. In the past China has built alliances and partnerships with countries in the Indian periphery, most notably Pakistan, but also Myanmar, Nepal, Sri Lanka, Bangladesh and, more recently, Afghanistan.[20]

The China-Pakistan-India Triangle

The future of Pakistan remains a key factor in the Sino-Indian relationship, and the future of Kashmir remains critical to the Indo-Pakistani relationship. Therefore any move by China that either intentionally or inadvertently secured gains for Pakistan on the Kashmir issue would invite much concern in India. For example, a recent decision by China to issue separate visas to residents of Indian-administered Kashmir led to a minor diplomatic stand-off. Such moves are, to be sure, contrary to the overall thrust of Chinese policy since the 1990s. Territorial integrity has occupied the minds of India's leaders ever since the country gained independence in 1947, when more than 500 princely states had to be incorporated into the Indian Union – a considerable task for any post-colonial state. Given this mindset, the Sino-Indian border conflict could prove particularly intractable. Since its formation, the People's Republic has settled its borders with a number of neighbours, often making concessions to the other party. The Indian border, however, remains contentious and a continuing source of ill will between the two nations. Initial formulations by Zhou Enlai in the 1950s had envisaged a quid pro quo settlement whereby India would drop its claims in the western sector in exchange for China's concession of the eastern sector.

Since the end of the Cold War, a fundamental shift of China's South Asia policy has been to take a more evenhanded approach in its relations with Pakistan and India and to make Sino-Pakistani and Sino-Indian relations independent of each other. It has been observed that of all China's relations with South Asian states, those with Pakistan outweigh and overlay any other bilateral relationship. No other Asian country has armed another in such a consistent manner over such a long period of time as China has armed Pakistan. The China–Pakistan type of nuclear/missile cooperation, in particular, is unprecedented in the history of post-1945 international relations. Even the United States and Britain did not share such a relationship. At Bandung, China is reported to have reached a 'strategic understanding with Pakistan founded on their convergent interests vis-à-vis

India'.[21]

After Bandung, the emerging competition between India and China contributed to an increasingly strained bilateral relationship that was soon put to the test in addressing a serious irritant: the Sino-Indian border. While some have traced the roots of the Indo-Chinese border dispute to a much earlier period,[22] its immediate antecedents lay in the Chinese invasion of Tibet in 1950. This created significant tensions in India, which had strategic interests in Tibet and 'spiritual bonds' with Tibetan civilisation stretching back almost two millennia.[23] Writing at the height of the Sino-Indian border conflict, P.C. Chakravarti expressed apprehensions: 'Any strong expansionist power, entrenched in Tibet, holds in its hands a loaded pistol pointed at the heart of India'.[24]

During his 1991 visit to New Delhi, Li Peng, the Chinese premier at the time, told reporters that "China is willing to maintain and develop friendly relations with India, Pakistan, and all countries in South Asia on the basis of the Five Principles of Peaceful Coexistence." The real message was that better ties between China and India should not affect China's links with Pakistan and that China's existing friendship and cooperation with Pakistan should not block improvement of Sino-Indian relations. Since then, China has established an all-weather strategic cooperative partnership with Pakistan and a strategic and cooperative partnership for peace and prosperity with India.

However, strong inertia persists, both inside and outside all three countries, in viewing the China-Pakistan-India triangle through the old-fashioned prism of confrontation, with China and Pakistan on one side and India on the other. Pakistan still hinders China-India relations, with India complaining of China's support for Pakistan in areas such as defense ties, civilian nuclear cooperation, and counter-terrorism. It is true that China is much closer strategically to Pakistan than to India, despite its much tighter economic links with India. China and Pakistan portray each other as brothers, while the China-India strategic partnership is still a work in progress. Also, a weaker Pakistan—suffering from economic difficulties, terrorist attacks, natural disasters, tensions with the United States, and increased strength inferiority to India—expects more support from China. The respective distrust between China and India and between China and the United States, and the strengthened Indo-U.S. strategic partnership has upgraded the significance to China of the China-Pakistan all-weather friendship. Therefore, before the final settlement of the protracted, unresolved China-India border dispute, China's friendship with Pakistan will remain an irritant to India's dealing with China. However, since China and India have agreed to look at their relationship in a broader context and perceive a stable and cooperative partnership as a guarantee to their simultaneous rise.

Pakistan as a Factor in India-China Relations

The most contentious issue for India is China's strategic relationship with Pakistan. India has always viewed the Sino-Pakistani relationship, particularly China's nuclear and missile assistance to Pakistan, as part of China's strategy to contain India's influencein South Asia. Over the years China and Pakistan have developed close tiesin the political and military spheres, including significant arms transfer aswell as nuclear and missile assistance. Traditionally, this assistance has been motivated by a number of considerations, the key elements being to promotea militarily capable Pakistan that would serve as a counterweight to a predominant India in the region, and Chinese military and trade access to the Arabian Sea. Chinese military help would also lessen the pressure on Chinato intervene on Pakistan's behalf should India and Pakistan get involved in amilitary conflict.

However, since the end of cold war, China's position has shifted from unequivocal support for Pakistan in the Kashmir dispute to the encouragement of India–Pakistan rapprochement. Though China's policy towards Pakistan has shifted towards neutrality to allow the improvement of India-China relations and avoid unnecessary entanglements, it is still willing to do the minimum necessary to preserve Pakistani security from a distance. Certainly China has no intentions todesert its long time ally and indeed substantial Chinese defence assistance to Pakistan continues. Contradictions between India-China-Pakistan relationships will continue to exist, but what matters is, whether the contradictions are "antagonistic" or non-antagonistic." The Beijing–Islamabad 'special relationship' is part of China's grand strategy that moulds the South Asian security environment. It provides a good example of using China as a counterweight to what smaller South Asian regimes perceive as India's attempts at bullying them. It demonstrates that much like Pakistan, other South Asian countries can follow an 'independent' policy and need not allow India to influence their decision making. Combined with the Chinese presence in the Indian Ocean region, this has created some concern among Indian policymakers of strategic encirclement.[25] China is investing heavily in Pakistan-held northern areas as well, with unconfirmed reports of troop presences. Also, the defense establishment in India, given the successive upgrade of the dual-use infrastructure projects and military deployments in Tibet, had elevated Indian threat perceptions from low to medium levels vis-a-vis China, although there is not yet a clear and present danger.

India and the Region

Southern Asia is India's closest and most vital sphere of strategic action. India's relations with many of its SouthAsian neighbors remain fraught, if not hostile. Political problems aside, there is a structural reason for such a state of affairs. India is by far the largest, most populous, and most powerful country in the region,where it accounts for 70 percent of population, nearly 80 percent of GDP, and about 75 percent of trade. Its conventional forces are the largest in the region. Moreover, India shares a boundary with every country in the neighborhood, but most of them do not share a border with another South Asian country. India's abilityto play a more engaged role on the global stage is contingent on its capacity for ensuring amodicum of stability in its relationships with sub-continental neighbors. Stability in its tieswith its Southern Asian neighbors remains a key geopolitical objective for India because "India will not be able to realize its own destiny without the partnership of its South Asian neighbours."

Further, India's economic ties with its sub-continental neighbors remain weak. South Asia is among the least integrated regions of the world. Official intra-regional trade, to take one indicator, hovers around 5 percent of total trade of the countries of the region. This is abysmally low not just in comparison to other regions of Asia (the corresponding figure for East Asia exceeds 50 percent), but also when contrasted with its own potential for growth through trade. South Asia has three attributes that make it extremely well-suited for integration by trade: the highest population density in the world; linguistic and ethnic overlap across borders; and the presence of a large number of cities close to the borders. This potential has not been adequately tapped for at least two reasons. One of the legacies of colonialism has been ambivalence about free trade in most South Asian countries. This problem was compounded by the economic and political consequences of partition, which not only set the stage for many protracted disputes but also overturned the political economy of the region. Before 1947, the region had an almost unimpeded flow of goods, money, people, and ideas. An integrated Southern Asian market would make eminent economic sense as well as help take the sting out of uneasy political relationships.

Finally, South Asia confronts a series of non-traditional security challenges, ranging from public health to migration to water. Environmental issues, in particular, pose serious problems for the region as a whole. The mountain and deltaic ecosystems of Southern Asia are closely integrated and cut across state boundaries. The region is unique in the sheer size of population, scarcity of rainfall, reliance on agriculture, scope for mega-dam projects, and vulnerability to climate change. Environmental and natural resource management will perhaps be the biggest and most potent challenge for the countries of Southern Asia. Climate change and changes inpatterns of resource use are also imposing strains on existing bilateral arrangements between India and its neighbors.

Further, new challenges are likely to arise from China's approach to dealing with environmental issues, especially water, in the Tibetan plateau. Until now, India has dealt with its neighbors over water issues as the upper riparian. But today, with China emerging as the key factor in this domain, India will have to work from a rather different vantage point. The challenge for India (and other South Asian states) is to move toward creating cooperative mechanisms fordealing with these common challenges.

Chinese Impact

The Sino-Indian war is often cited as a watershed moment in Indian foreign policy, after which Nehruvian idealism began to give way to the pragmatic impulses of subsequent administrations. After the war, India began to align itself more closely with the Soviet Union, which had begun to split from China within the international Communist movement; meanwhile, China and Pakistan developed closer ties. In 1964, China conducted its first nuclear test, at Lop Nor, which provided impetus for India's own successful 'peaceful' nuclear test at Pokhran ten years later. The 1965 India–Pakistan war was a litmus test of the already established US–Pakistan relationship as well as the new Sino-Pakistani relationship. When the United States declared neutrality and blocked military transfers to both India and Pakistan, Islamabad turned to Beijing for assistance, which it provided in generous quantities. When war broke out, China came down heavily on Pakistan's side and threatened to open a front with India on the Sikkim border. US diplomatic intervention and a United Nations resolution calling for a ceasefire were ultimately necessary to discourage Chinese intervention.

Indeed, over the past five decades China has regarded Pakistan as a useful counterweight to India in South Asia. The relationship with Pakistan has enabled Beijing to pursue an Indias trategy on the cheap, while maintaining its own focus on other areas of more immediate interest. There is little reason to believe that China will abandon this approach any time soon, and there is some reason to believe that the strategic relationship with Pakistan mightactually be tightening. China is, of course, concerned about instability and extremism in Pakistan. Terrorism is on the agenda of the strategic dialogue between China and India.

On the economic front, though, China could potentially play a positive role. There is some evidence to suggest that the recent moves by Pakistan toward granting most-favored-nation status to India may have been quietly encouraged by China. Two factors seem to be at workhere. The strains in Pakistan's relations with the United States and the impending U.S. troop drawdown in Afghanistan are likely to result in a gradual erosion of American aid to Pakistan. China, however, seems unwilling to fill the breach all by itself and would like to see Pakistan's economy standing on its own feet. Further, China's advice to Pakistan is consonant with the manner in which its own relationship with India has evolved over the past two decades.

India's relations with China are a complex amalgam of elements of competition and cooperation. Economic ties between India and China have burgeoned in recent years. Yet this relationship remains asymmetric, with a mounting trade surplus in China's favor. Politically, the two countries have found it easier to work together on global issues such as climate change, and in areas such as the BRICS (the developing economies of Brazil, Russia, andSouth Africa in addition to India and China). Yet, the core bilateral dispute on the boundaries remains unresolved. On the security front, the peace and tranquility agreements havehelped avoid military standoffs along the disputed borders. Yet, the gap between the overall military capabilities has widened in China's favor, as to a lesser extent have the local military balances along the borders.

Thus New Delhi is attempting to gain greater market access in China for Indian firms, while encouraging Chinese firms to invest in India, especially in infrastructure; to try to workwith China on areas of mutual interest on multilateral and global forums, while pursuing apolitical dialogue to settle the boundary dispute; to enhance military confidence-building measures, while working toward upgrading its military capabilities along the borders and developing a maritime strategy that will play to India's strengths in the Indian Ocean region and beyond. In a nutshell, India aims for the normalization of its ties with China while trying to curb China's ability to impinge on its geopolitical space and interests. If India's relationship with Pakistan has complicated itsties with China, it is mainly due to the manner in which China has sought to use Pakistan vis-a-vis India. China's support for Pakistan, especially in the military and nuclear domains, remains a matter of serious concern for India. Ideally, India would like to de-link its relationship with China and with Pakistan. But this does not seem a realistic prospect in the foreseeable future. Indeed, if Pakistan's dependence on China increases in the years ahead, New Delhi may have to start thinking about Pakistan as a subset of the larger challenges posed by China. Perhaps the biggest challenge to Sino-Indian rapprochement, and a source of impetus, is the rapidly improving US–Indian relationship. While a much-improved relationship with Washington has helped India counter the traditional pro-Pakistan tilt in US foreign policy, it has also made Sino-Indian rapprochement a greater priority for Beijing.[26]

Ultimately, neither China nor India stands to gain from sparking a regional conflict. Both nations are deeply engaged in the domestic sphere, including generating economic reform, maintaining state legitimacy and juggling ethno-nationalism. Even the ostensible machinations of the United States have done little to hamper the current upswing in Sino-Indian relations. In some key international forums, including those addressing climate changes, trade, labour laws, arms control and human rights, China and India have found common ground in countering Western positions, though their tactical alliances have often proved unstable in the heat of negotiation. The unconnected nature of China's and India's rise is striking. Bilateral trade, while growing fast, is a small share of overall trade for both countries. Major strategic partnerships have been made with third parties, including Pakistan and the United States. Societal interaction between the two nationsis still negligible, though tourism is growing and interpersonal connections related to trade between the two countries are also increasing. Direct flights between India and China, however, only began in 2002, and in 2007, thetwo nations, with a combined population of over 2 billion, exchanged apaltry 570,000 visitors.[27]

In the absence of single and inclusive security

architecture in Asia, many security challenges in Asia remain unresolved or even un attended. In this background, India's security challenges are no different from those of many Asian countries. Three pressing security challenges that India faces today are included in the traditional and nontraditional security domains: unresolved sovereignty and territorial disputes; terrorism; and maintaining economic growth in light of the global financial crisis andeuro-zone crisis on the one hand and the rising cost of energy, food, and other commodities on the other hand.

China and India have already attained regional power status. Both are unable to reassert their traditional suzerainty over their smaller neighbours, as anyattempt to do so encounter resistance from regional and extra-regional powers. Both claimthat their attitude towards their neighbours is essentially benevolent while making it clearthese neighbours must not make policies or take actions, or allow other nations to takemeasures in their territory, which they deem to be against their own interest and security. Both accuse each other of pursuing hegemony and entertaining imperial ambitions.

The root cause of the volatile and strained Sino–Indian relationship, therefore, lies in Beijing's determination to prevent India from playing a role it once played as a civilisation and empire from Central Asia to Southeast Asia, and in New Delhi's counter-containment strategies. If China can justify nuclear/missile assistance to Pakistan as part of 'normal state-to-state relations', so could India to its 'all-weather friends', Vietnam and Mongolia. After all, China has not taken out an exclusive patent ontrade in nuclear/ missile technologies.[28]

Despite steadily improving relations with India since the late 1980s, China has not becomeless friendly to Pakistan, primarily because the combined strategic and political advantages China receives from its relationship with

Pakistan (and, through Pakistan, other Islamic countries) easily outweigh any advantages China might receive from a closer relationship with India. Above all, Pakistan is the only country that stands up to India and thereby prevents Indian hegemony over the region, thus fulfilling the key objective of China's South Asia policy. The Chinese believe that as long as India is preoccupied with Pakistan on itswestern frontier, it will not stir up trouble on the Tibetan border. A secure and stable India at peace with Pakistan would, on the other hand, make New Delhi focus on China and East Asia. Such a move would spell the virtual end to Chinese aspirations of being the leading Asian power and would greatly weaken China's position against Indian power. It was the provision of the Chinese nuclear and missiles hield to Pakistan during the late 1980s and 1990s (at the height of China–India rapprochement) that emboldened Islamabad to wage a proxy war in Kashmir. Because, by helping Pakistan to emerge as a nuclear power, China has created realistic long-term security problem for India. The strategic parity with India that Pakistan has given it tremendous potential to emerge as a major factor in Southwest and Central Asia, if it couldset its economy in order.[29]

A staunch ally such as Pakistan also provides China with asecure access to naval bases (Karachi, Ormara and Gwader) close to the entrance of the Persian Gulf. Furthermore, Beijing's concerns about separatist Islamic influence in its far-western region of Xinjiang also explain China's indulgence towards Pakistan. China apparently feels strongly that engaging Pakistan's government, and even its fundamentalist religious parties, is an important part of keeping control in its own restive Muslim northwest.

Pakistan remains a major recipient of Chinese largesse. While Pakistan continues to be a useful instrument of Chinese foreign policy in South Asia and the Persian Gulf, one cannot rule out the possibility of the pragmatic Chinese evaluating their policy towards Pakistan, but this will happen only if Pakistan's slow descent into chaos and anarchy continues unabated. Talibanisation of Pakistani state and society during the 1990s has, however, created some frictions between Beijing and Islamabad. Nor can Beijing turn a blind eye to the activities of *jihadi* parties based in Afghanistan and Pakistan. The experts in the subject admit that 'China has some problems with Pakistan' over its deep involvement with the Taliban regime in Afghanistan and the 'export of fundamentalist Islamic political ideas'.[30]

Conclusion

The analysis of the events indicates that security concerns and the state of Sino–Indian relations impact heavily on China's relations with South Asian countries. The Chinese areat pains to emphasise that the improvement and development of Sino–Indian relations will by no means adversely affect the existing friendly relations between China and other South Asian countries. Current strategic and economictrends indicate that South Asia's importance in China's national security calculus is likely to increase in the twenty-first century.

The relationship between India and China is at a crossroads at the beginning of the third millennium. While there are many similarities in Chinese and Indian strategic cultures, nothing illustrates differences better than the fact that China has emerged as a hardware superpower while India has emerged as a software superpower in the new 'knowledge economy'. Historic rivalries and their strategic cultures suggest that a fair amount of tension between these continent-sized neighbours, which also happen to be the world's two most populous nations, is inevitable. In the international status stakes, it is China with which India wants to achieve parity. India and China share similar aspirations towards status and influence, with China further advanced towards their achievement than India.

Although China and India are likely to remain long-term, if not permanent, adversaries, their aspirations appear to be manageable. India and Chinaneed not resort to use of force to neutralise each other's aspirations. The restoration of Tibet's autonomy, and a peaceful resolution of the Kashmir dispute could be powerfulmitigating factors in Sino–Indian rivalry. The problem, for both the Chinese and their neighbours, is to find the balance point of common interests where security can be achieved for all. Otherwise, China and India will remain locked in competition for political, economic and strategic supremacy with all the potentially destabilising consequences for regional security in southern Asia.[31]

References

1. Swaran Singh, 'Sino–South Asian Ties: Problems & Prospects', *Strategic Analysis* (New Delhi), 24,1 (2000), p. 31.
2. John W. Garver, 'China and South Asia', *Annals of the American Academy of Political and Social Science*, 519 (1992), p. 79.
3. 'ibid', p. 73.
4. Amitabh Mattoo, 'Shadow of the Dragon', in Gary K. Bertsch, S. Gahlaut and A. Srivastava (eds), *Engaging India* (New York and London: Routledge, 1999), pp. 219–220.
5. Austin Coates, *China, India and the Ruins of Washington* (New York, John Day, 1972), p. 293.
6. Mohan Malik, 'Nuclear Proliferation in Asia: The China Factor', *Australian Journal of International Affairs*, 53,1 (1999), p. 37.
7. Mohan Malik 'Burma's Role in Regional Security', in Morten B. Peterson, Emily Rudland and R. J. May (eds), *Burma Myanmar: Strong Regime Weak State?* (London and Adelaide, C. Hurst and Crawford House, 2000), pp. 241–277.
8. Ye Zhengjia, 'Sino–Indian Relations in the Last Five Decades:

Experiences and Lessons', *International Studies* (Beijing), 12–14 (1999), pp. 17–27.

9. Shao Chuan Leng, 'India and China', *Far Eastern Survey*, vol. 21, no. 8, 21 May 1952, pp. 73–8.
10. Waheguru Pal Singh Sidhu and Jing-dong Yuan, *China and India: Cooperation or Conflict?* (Boulder, CO: Lynne Rienner, 2003), p. 17.
11. Shekhar Gupta, 'Stop Fighting the 1962 War', *Indian Express*, 19 September 2009.
12. Michael H. Hunt, *The Genesis of Chinese Communist Foreign Policy* (New York: Columbia University Press, 1996), p. 16.
13. Sidhu Waheguru Pal Singh and Yuan Jing-dong. China and India- Cooperation or Conflict, India Research Press, New Delhi, 2003. pp. 151-152.
14. Documents of the 16th National Congress of the Communist Party of China [Zhongguo Gongchandang Dishiliuci Quanguodabiao Dahui Wenjian Huibian], (Beijing, China: Foreign Language Press, 2002), 2.
15. China's Document About the Position of the New Security Concept [Zhongguo Guanyu Xin Anquanguan Lichang De Wenjian], put forward by the Chinese delegation at the meeting of ASEAN Regional Forum (ARF), held in Seri Begawan, Brunei, July 31, 2002; see People's Daily, August 2, 2002), 3.
16. Chinese Ambassador Hu Xiaodi's Speech at the Conference on Disarmament in Geneva, February 7, 2002.
17. "China's National Defense in 2008 (White Paper)," Information Office of the State Council of the People's Republic of China, January 2009.
18. Arun Shourie, 'Digging Our Head Deeper in the Sand', *Indian Express*, 7 April 2009.
19. 'Olympic Torch Will Be Safe Here, India Assures China', *Indian Express*, 27 March 2008.

20. Thomas Adams and Arnav Manchanda, 'The Dragon in the Hindu Kush: China's Interests in Afghanistan', *Globe and Mail*, 20 April 2009.
21. John W. Garver, *Protracted Contest: Sino-Indian Rivalry in the Twentieth Century* (Seattle, WA: University of Washington Press, 2001), p. 5.
22. Xuecheng Liu, *The Sino-Indian Border Dispute and Sino-Indian Relations* (Lanham, MD: University Press of America, 1994), p. 12.
23. Mohan Guruswamy and Zorawar Daulet Singh, *India China Relations: The Border Issue and Beyond* (New Delhi: Viva Books, 2009), p. 38.
24. P.C. Chakravarti, 'Introduction', in *India–China Relations* (Calcutta: Firma K.L. Mukhopadhyay, 1961).
25. Steven Hoffmann, 'Perception and China Policy', in Frankel and Harding (eds), *The India–China Relationship*, p. 48.
26. C. Raja Mohan, *Crossing the Rubicon: The Shaping of India's New Foreign Policy* (New Delhi: Viking, 2003), p. 163.
27. Alka Acharya, *China and India: Politics of Incremental Engagement* (New Delhi: Har-Anand, 2008), p. 15.
28. Brahma Chellaney, 'No Syrupy Sentiment, Please', *Hindustan Times* (17 May 2000); 'Twin Timing China', *Hindustan Times* (14 June 2000).
29. Ehsan Ahrari, 'Nuclearised South Asia Faces an Uncertain Future', *Asia–Pacific Defence Reporter* (December 1999), p. 19.
30. Nayan Chanda and Susan Lawrence, 'Nuclear Balancing Act', *Far Eastern Economic Review* (16 March 2000), pp. 26–27. Also see Mohan Malik, 'Pakistan: Front Line, Fault Line', *The World Today*, 56,2 (2000), pp. 14–16.
31. Andrew J. Nathan and Robert S. Ross, *The Great Wall and the Empty Fortress: China's Search for Security* (New York and London: W.W. Norton, 1997), p. 231.

9

Changing Dynamics of India China Relations in Covid Era

Dr. Swati Thakur

Introduction

India and China are perceived as Asian giants by several scholars around the globe. Both are geographically and demographically huge countries with enormous potential to be big powers. They also share a bitter past. As a result they are weighed against each other as competitors and potential opponents. However, they were not always pitted against each other. India and China attained their independence in the year 1947 and 1949 respectively. The very next year, in 1950, India established diplomatic relations with China, making her the first non communist country which officially recognised the People's Republic of China[1].

Assistant Professor, Department of Political Science and Public Administration, Dr. Shakuntala Misra National Rehabilitation University, Lucknow

The year 1954 was the landmark year in the relations between India and China, Premiers Nehru and Zhou Enlai paid their mutual visits and proposed the well-known Five Principles of Peaceful Co-existence or Panchsheel[2]. This bonhomie was soon replaced by tensions, mistrust, bitterness and mutual suspicion due to a number of factors like power politics of the Cold War era and the exile of His Holiness the Dalai Lama in India. The full scale war between India and China in 1962 marked the lowest point in the relations between the two neighbours resulting in perpetual tension on the Sino-Indian border. After almost three decades Indian Prime Minister Rajiv Gandhi made an attempt to restore the ties. After the end of the Cold War, several bilateral visits by Indian and Chinese Premiers took place, which tried to strengthen and expand the relations. However, areas of conflict persisted. According to the Neo realist school, conflict and competition between India and China is inevitable as "one mountain cannot accommodate two tigers."[3] This view appears to be relevant in the time when the spread of the corona virus pandemic has brought about profound changes in international relations. It has its impact on the India China relations like never before. In Order to understand the changing dynamics of India China relations in Covid era we need to throw some light on the India relation with China just before the pandemic.

Chinese Foreign Policy under Xi Jinping

In the year 2018, Chinese Parliament amended the constitution removing the two term limit for the President. This allowed Xi Jinping to remain President for life. Xi Jinping has amassed powers which have not been seen in history since Mao Zedong[4]. Xi Jinping has crafted a foreign and domestic policy according to his own vision. The Chinese foreign policy has undergone sea change under President Xi Jinping. Foreign policy under Xi Jinping marks a significant departure from the past and sets the tone for an ambitious and assertive role in world affairs. In the 19th National Party Congress of the Communist Party of China (CPC), held in October 2017, President Xi Jinping expressed his vision of China leading in International affairs. He said that the Chinese Nation has stood up, grown rich, and become stronger. He further added that China is moving close to the center stage and making greater contributions to mankind. In this speech he further said that China would endeavor to uphold international fairness and justice, and oppose acts that impose one's will on others or interfere in the internal affairs of others as well as the practice of the strong bullying the weak[5]. This statement clearly shows a desire for an important role in world affairs.

China being a global leader means that the Chinese economy would lead the world. Xi Jinping has highlighted this fact in his address to the CPC in 2017. He said that China will expand foreign trade, develop new models and new forms of trade. This would turn China into a trader of quality. Explaining further he said that China would adopt policies to promote high-standard liberalization and facilitation of trade and investment. China would implement the system of pre-establishment national treatment plus a negative list across the board, significantly ease market access, further open the service sector, and protect the legitimate rights and interests of foreign investors, promote trade and investment liberalization and facilitation, and make economic globalization more open, inclusive, and balanced so that its benefits are shared by all. It clearly means that China aims to dominate and control the supply chain across the world to become a big power. Xi Jinping came up with the ambitious idea of Belt and Road Initiative (BRI).

The Belt and Road initiative is a dream project of Xi Jinping's ambitious foreign policy. It is roughly modeled on the pattern of Silk route of ancient period, which connected China, Central Asia and areas of modern day Pakistan and

India. Importance of the Silk route in history lies in the fact that it connected eastern and western markets, spurring immense wealth, and intermixing cultural and religious traditions[6]. Xi Jinping announced the BRI in the year 2013. The BRI plan was two-pronged: the overland Silk Road Economic Belt and the Maritime Silk Road. The two were collectively referred to first as the One Belt, One Road initiative but eventually became the Belt and Road Initiative[7]. Under the overland scheme of BRI, China plans to create a vast network of railways, energy pipelines, highways, and streamlined border crossings, both westward—through the former Soviet republics—and southward, to Pakistan, India, and the rest of Southeast Asia. This would expand the international use of Chinese currency thus increasing Chinese power. Under the maritime scheme, Xi Jinping plans to invest in port development along the Indian Ocean, from the South China Sea, Southeast Asia all the way to East Africa and parts of Europe. BRI fulfills the geopolitical and economic ambitions of China. China has invested a huge amount in this project. It has formalized agreements with more than sixty countries around the globe to invest in infrastructure, trade and finance of these countries. China- Pakistan Economic Corridor (CPEC) is one of the examples of BRI.

Another important component of power in Chinese foreign policy besides economy is the military. It would not be wrong to say that the direct outcome of Chinese economic growth is modernization of its military. In recent years, particularly under the leadership of Xi Jinping, efforts have been made to restructure the organization of armed forces. A lot of attention is paid to strengthen military training and war preparedness. This has been done to protect the maritime interest and overseas aspirations of China. In recent years Chinese exercise of hegemony is clearly visible in Hong Kong, Taiwan and South China Sea and currently on the Indian border with China.

Impact of Xi Jinping Foreign Policy on India

Seeds of distrust were sown between India and China way back in time of Mao Zedong. Mao considered Tibet to be China's right-hand palm, with five fingers – Bhutan, Nepal and the three Indian territories of Ladakh, Arunachal Pradesh and Sikkim. The five fingers were also to be "liberated." In the 1962 war against India, China gained a sizeable territory in Ladakh, the Aksai Chin plateau[8]. With this background Xi Jinping's dream of powerful China, particularly the Belt Road Initiative made India uneasy.

Ever since the launch of BRI in 2013, India has opposed it vehemently. India perceives this project as a malicious design by China to assert its hegemony. India has tried to convince countries that the BRI is a plan to dominate Asia. It is seen as a geo-economic strategy by China to create unsustainable debt burdens for its Indian Ocean neighbors in order to seize control of regional choke points. CPEC is seen by India as a grand alliance forged by China alongside Pakistan to challenge Indian position in South Asia.

Though India was aware of China's intentions India tried to avoid any kind of confrontation with China. The Modi Government in its initial years tried to engage China on several multilateral forums like BRICS and WTO. Economic cooperation was promoted by both the countries. Prime Minister Modi later tried to engage China bilaterally. He said, "Asia and the world will have a better future when India and China work together with trust and confidence[9]" Prime Minister Modi has tried to engage China formally and informally on several occasions. In Spite of the cordial atmosphere that the meeting generated, tensions mistrust and suspicion persisted.

The spread of the corona virus pandemic has shaken the international system. It has changed the dynamics of India-China relations.

Covid and the Changing Dynamics

The Corona virus pandemic also known as Covid 19 has its impact on all the countries around the world. It is not just a medical situation. It has its deep impact on world affairs. Covid 19 has created a power vacuum in International affairs. There has been a complete lack of leadership at global level to tackle the crisis. Every country, big or small, super power or emerging power is seen struggling to cope with the spread and impact of the corona virus.

Covid has also redefined the concept of power. The pandemic has proved that a nation cannot become powerful relying on the economy and military alone. In the current scenario the military looks irrelevant and nations are struggling to sustain their economies. Today the Health sector has become an important constituent of power. Now countries need to focus on the internal infrastructure to survive. China seems to have done well in restricting the corona virus cases as compared to India and America. This crisis has exposed the dependency of Indian pharmaceutical industry on China. India's pharmaceutical sector sources a majority of its Advanced Pharmaceutical Ingredients from China.

The hyper interconnectivity of the pre covid era was one the reason for the fast spread of the virus all over the world. As a result borders all across the world had to be shut. Not only had the borders between the countries but the lockdown within the countries brought the internal movement to a standstill. This situation has a direct impact on the Belt and Road Initiative. There has been delays and disruption due to quarantine and containment measures. A slowdown is expected to persevere in the near future as countries experiment with different levels of lockdown amidst uncertainty about future surges. The economic expenditure on BRI has increased many folds.

Since the virus originated from China, it is being

blamed for mismanagement, lack of transparency which resulted in the spread of the pandemic all over the world. Pandemic has severely damaged China's international reputation resulting in alienation of its partners. America openly blamed China for the crisis. President Trump even went to the extent of calling corona virus, China Virus. International criticism has not gone down well with China. It has made China more aggressive. Chinese diplomats have taken to Twitter and other social media to counter-attack any criticism of its handling of the pandemic, or on any other issue. The language used is often crude and offensive[10]. China is now pursuing 'wolf warrior diplomacy'. The term wolf warrior has been derived from a Chinese movie by the same name released in the year 2015. The tagline of the movie says "Even though a thousand miles away, anyone who affronts China will pay." This is the approach that China has adopted towards India and the world.

The adoption of wolf warrior diplomacy by China against India is changing the dynamics of India-China relations. No matter how hard the pandemic has hit the world, China is using it as an opportunity to assert its hegemony in the region. In the month of May, India-China border witnessed tensions along the Line of Actual Control (LAC). In the face off between the two sides several soldiers lost their lives. This has been the worst crisis in almost forty years. The stand-off in Galwan valley, according to reports, was triggered by China moving in troops and equipment to stop construction activity by India. According to India, this was well within India's side of the LAC. Not only in Ladakh, but Chinese army has been gradually building up in the Arunachal Pradesh border. The territorial claims made by each side defy easy resolution. China is also escalating the situation by laying claim to territory under Bhutan's control. Beijing is claiming Sakteng Wildlife Sanctuary in eastern Bhutan—close to the Indian state of Arunachal Pradesh.

Xi Jinping, while adopting wolf warrior diplomacy, it appears, is working to complete Mao's expansionist vision. Mao's China annexed Xinjiang and Tibet, more than doubling the country's territory and making it the world's fourth largest by area. Its annexation of resource-rich Tibet, in particular, represented one of the most far-reaching geopolitical developments in post-World War II history, not least because it gave China common borders with India, Nepal, Bhutan, and northern most Myanmar[11]. Intentions of China are very clear. China wants to dominate the world. Not only India, but several countries are realizing the ulterior Chinese motives. Covid pandemic as has brought about significant geo strategic changes in South Asia.

Conclusion

Covid pandemic has brought about significant changes in the dynamics of India China relations. Relations between India and China had not been cordial for a long time. But this is the first time in many years that relations have hit a nadir. Covid has exposed the growing imbalance between India-China relations. China is emerging as a big power. Today, the health care sector has become an important element of power. While India is one of worst hit countries by the pandemic, China has successfully managed the pandemic situation. Indian pharmaceutical industry is heavily dependent on China. Perhaps this pandemic will serve as a wakeup call for a more self reliant pharmaceutical industry.

Though China was badly hit by the pandemic, it is also the first country which is showing signs of recovery. It has become more arrogant and assertive with its wolf warrior diplomacy. It has consistently undermined India's vital interests in various international organizations, territorial sovereignty, border conflict, counter global terrorism, expanded maritime policies in the Indian Ocean and South China Sea. The recent Chinese encroachment in the LAC and the subsequent clashes between the two armies are a dangerous signal. China's ambitious BRI has encircled India. CPEC and the growing tilt of Nepal towards China are changing the dynamics between the two countries further. India has adopted the right approach of engaging the Quadrilateral Security Dialogue or the Quad. Quad is a group of four countries Australia, India, Japan, and the United States. India hosted a Quad ministerial meeting during the pandemic. Currently these four countries together are trying to counter Chinese aggression.

There is no doubt that the dynamics have changed in the pandemic time.The post covid period will witness a new alignments and a new power structure where both, India and China will play an important role.

References

1. Guihong, Z.(2012). The shifting Balance of Power and China – India Relations: Between Cooperation and competition, In Devare,S.T., Singh,S., Marwah,R.(Eds), Emerging China: Prospects for Partnership in Asia, New Delhi, Routledge, p 320
2. Guihong, Z.(2012). The shifting Balance of Power and China – India Relations: Between Cooperation and competition, In Devare, S.T., Singh, S., Marwah, R.(Eds), Emerging China: Prospects for Partnership in Asia, New Delhi, Routledge, p 320
3. Athwal, A.(2008). China – India Relations: Contemporary Dynamics, New York, Rouledge, p 2
4. *https://www.bbc.com/news/world-asia-china-43361276*
5. *http://www.xinhuanet.com/english/download/Xi_Jinping's_ report_ at_19th_CPC_National_Congress.pdf*
6. *https://www.cfr.org/backgrounder/chinas-massive-belt-and-road-initiative*
7. *https://www.cfr.org/backgrounder/chinas-massive-belt-and-road-initiative*

8. Brahma, C. China's expansionist agenda takes shape on the Indian border, the globe and mail, published august 31, 2020

9. *https://www.orfonline.org/research/modis-new-china-policy/*

10. Shyam Saran, the Print , 1st June 2020

11. *https://www.project-syndicate.org/commentary/china-xi-resurrects-mao-five-fingers-strategy-by-brahma-chellaney-2020-07*

10

India- China Relations: Especially with reference to NDA Government

Dr. Neelam Gupta

On the 70th anniversary of Sino-India relation, it is particularly important to revisit the original aspiration of establishing diplomatic relations. The rhetoric jingle 'Hindi-Chini Bhai-Bhai' never really bloomed although the China –India relations kept moving ahead despite wind and rain.

The modern relationship began in 1950 when India was among the first countries to end formal ties with the Republic of China (Taiwan) and recognized the People's Republic of China as the legitimate government of Mainland China. China and India are the two most populous countries and fastest growing major economies in the world. Growth in diplomatic and economic influence has increased the significance of their bilateral relationship. Cultural and economic relations between China and India date back to ancient times. The Silk Road not only served as a major trade

Deptt of Political Science, Bareilly College, Bareilly(U.P.)

route between India and China, but is also credited for facilitating the spread of Buddhism from India to East Asia.[1] During the 19th century, China's growing opium trade with the British East India Company triggered the First and Second Opium Wars.[2] During World War II, British-occupied India and China both played a crucial role in halting the progress of Imperial Japan.[3]

The Panchsheel doctrine was established in 1954 by India's Prime Minister Jawaharlal Nehru and the then Chinese Prime Minister Chou En Lai for co-existence and cooperation between the two countries. The five principles of Panchsheel included respect for each other's integrity and sovereignty, non-aggression, equality, peaceful co-existence and non-interference in each other's internal affairs, butthe relations between contemporary China and India have been characterized by border disputes, resulting in three military conflicts – the Sino-Indian War of 1962, the Chola incident in 1967, and the 1987 Sino-Indian skirmish.[4] In early 2017, the two countries clashed at the Doklam plateau along the disputed Sino-Bhutanese border.[5] However, since the late 1980s, both countries have successfully rebuilt diplomatic and economic ties. In 2008, China became India's largest trading partner and the two countries have ended up extending their strategic and military relations.[6] Apart from trade and commerce, there are some other areas of mutual interest on which China and India have been cooperating of late. In the words of Rejaul Karim Laskar, a scholar of Indian foreign policy, "Currently, the two countries are cooperating on a range of international like trade, climate change and reform of the global financial order, among others, to promote common interest"[7]

Sino-Indian relations had remained frozen after the 1962 War till 1976 when diplomatic activity restarted. Though the two sides resumed designating ambassadors to each other in 1976 after a long break, the real breakthrough came with the late prime minister Rajiv Gandhi's visit to China in 1988.It was historic because the Prime minister of India was visiting China after more than three decades*. The two sides agreed that pending resolution of the boundary dispute, they would maintain peace and tranquility along the Line of Actual Control (LAC), and make efforts to improve and develop bilateral relations. Since then, India and China have signed a number of agreements.

In April, 1999 the NDA, a new coalition led by the BJP gained majority to form the government with Atal Bihari Vajpayee as Prime Minister on October, 1999. The reorientation of the Indian foreign policy during the early 1990s and at the beginning of the 21st century under the Vajpayee government, was response to the changes within the international system after the end of cold war. It was in this context that the NDA government conducted two rounds of nuclear tests on 13th and 14th May, 1998 respectively. China was vocal opponent of India's nuclear test and made a strong point that the nuclear tests were against the international trend and was detrimental to the peace and stability of the South Asian region. Prior to the conducting of 1998 nuclear tests, George Fernandez, the then Defense Minister of India declared that China is India's number one threat. The message he wanted to convey to the international community was that India had developed nuclear weapons in defense against China's arsenal.

After some time, the Sino-Indian relations once again came back on the track of normalization. The two sides officially resumed talks in February, 1999 after a gap of months. During the BJP led NDA government's tenure, one of the important aims of India's foreign policy was to settle the border issue with China. In order to accelerate the talks on boundary issue, the Indian Foreign Minister Mr. Jaswant Singh visited China in 1999. He accelerated the pace of talks on the clarification of the Line of Actual Control (LAC).

There was agreement on promoting Confidence Building Measures (CBM's) thereby initiating security dialogue and expanding economic and trade relations. During his China visit, he made it clear that India does not consider China as a threat to it. Thus, his China visit created a friendly atmosphere in the deteriorating relations which have developed after the post nuclear tests. Thereafter, the President of India Mr. K.R. Narayan paid a visit to China on May, 2000. This was considered as an important visit because it was the first visit by a highest level leader. Sino-India relations further improved following Indian Prime Minister Atal Bihari Vajpayee's landmark visit to China in June, 2003. During his China visit, twelve agreements were signed which were expected to make Sino-India relations more cordial and friendly. The boundary issue which had always been an obstacle in building trust was overshadowed by the issues relating to trade and commerce.

Another important decision was taken, the Special Representatives (SRs) mechanism for resolution of the boundary dispute was also set up. India has shown readiness from this point of view and Brijesh Mishra, Principal Secretary to the Prime Minister, has been made special envoy for this task. Apart from the border dispute, both countries have made many important agreements on Vajpayee's visit on trade, education, visas and information technology, etc. Even more important and primary step than this agreement is that India will not believe that now both will not be a threat to each other. Since then, the SRs have had 22 rounds of talks (the last one in December, 2019) but without getting any closer to a resolution of the boundary dispute[8].

The BJP led NDA Government showed more flexibility in its foreign policy when Prime Minister Atal Bihari Vajpayee recognized Tibet Autonomous Region (TAR) as an inalienable part of China. India was expecting that in return, China should also recognize Sikkim as an Indian State, but, the

Chinese did not recognized Sikkim as an integral part of India. Here, it becomes clear that, This double strategy China's foreign policy with regard to India was based on both engagement and balance of power. Instead of all this, a common manifesto for mutual relations was broadened, along with an agreement to expand trade with border traders.

The two countries also signed a trade related MoU and nine agreements. The reality is that the economic and business future of both countries will be determined in the true sense by the political and diplomatic environment. The International Trade Promotion Council, in association with India's top industry body FICCI, has launched a guide book and website to gain and understand each other's market as quickly as possible. Along with this, road-map maps have also been prepared for the exchange of business information.

India-China relations are entering in a new era, which is a very important and timely initiative from a business and economic point of view, China has expressed a desire to invest $ 500 million in infrastructure development and resources in India. The two countries have also agreed to set up an action plan for economic cooperation, China has also approved the opening of 'Nathula Pass' for border trade to Sikkim and China's trade center in Sikkim's 'Chhangu' and Tibet. In 'Reniggoug', it has been agreed to set up an Indian trade post. Historically, Nathula has been a very important border from time immemorial in respect of trade. Along with this, the duration of business visas has also been extended, although there has been a mutual disagreement over trade relations that are filling India's market with its cheap goods, but India cares about it as an integral part of this phase of globalization. Happily did not hesitate to accept it as well.

India's border dispute with China is a chronic disease whose treatment is not immediately possible in any copy. No meaningful and clear policy has been formulated so far with regard to the elimination of the boundary of 14 attempts made during the last 22 years. It is also noteworthy that China has ended its border disputes with Pakistan, Nepal, Bhutan and Myanmar and land and disputes with Russia, Kazakhstan and Vietnam have also been stopped. China remains the only border disputes with India.

The best border between India and China, which is about 4056 km, is from Myanmar to Bhutan in three regions-Eastern regions Arunachal Pradesh, Lipulekh Pass in Shipki Pass of Central Nepal and Ladakh to Karakoram Pass in western region of Jammu and Kashmir. A large part of the eastern region was annexed by China during the 1962 war. But after the ceasefire, he went on the previous chariot, but he has claimed his entire area of about 90,000 square kilometers in the state. The eastern region has a border of 1100 kilometers, called the McMahon Line, which separates Arunachal from Tibet. Under this, about 5000 km of land is disputed, the 1600 km long Jammu and Kashmir border line between the two countries in the western region connects China with the areas of Sikyang and Tibet.

It has a disputed area of about 25,000 square kilometers, including Aksai China, adjacent to Pemong, and Aksai Chin and Ching Henam Valley adjacent to Ching Lake. Pakistan has given our 5180 square kilometers of land in Pakistan Occupied Kashmir under illegal soaps to China under the so-called Sino-Pak Agreement. The central region has a border line of about 650 km, which separates the mountainous regions of Spiti Varahoti and Nilang in the Himalayas. An area of 1600 square kilometers is disputed under this. The problem is actually more about the actual control line than what the Chinese are facing about the border of the eastern region. Surprising but true that the Chinese army attempted to forcefully enter Arunachal Pradesh even when Vajpayee was on a visit to China for the India-China talks. After limited surrender in this development, India withdrew 15 posts, Chinese soldiers also surrounded the paramilitary personnel and the Intelligence Bureau staff by filming, defying and carrying weapons and made a video film of surrender, which is natural to doubt China's intentions.

In the context of Sikkim too, China has made it clear that it has not even recognized the recognition of it as a part of India. Along with the border dispute, China's strategic attachment to Pakistan has been causing deviations in the Indo-China trust. Security concerns arising out of modern weapons being given by China to Pakistan are the real problem of mistrust. In Pakistan, China has not only built a route for its army to the Arabian Sea by constructing the Karakoram Highway, but it has also made a unique attempt by China to connect the Nepal border with the highway.

From the Chinese side, Sikkim is being counted as a very sensitive state because it is adjacent to the northeastern states. Northeast militants have been receiving arms and training from China. Therefore, as soon as China enters Sikkim in the name of border trade, there is no possibility of additional burden on Indian security system to be denied. There is a lot of barrier between their friendships over the India-China border dispute. China has been deliberately neglecting to resolve the border dispute with India, which is not a good sign in terms of relations.

This is what China has on the other hand amicably settled the border dispute with other neighbors, especially Russia. Not only this, China has been supplying its modern weapons and advanced nuclear technology to Pakistan as part of a planned strategy to rein in India. Pakistan's cooperation and China's ongoing strategic and tactical activities around India give us bittersweet signs to be vigilant. In any case, India and China will have to settle the boundary dispute and have to agree on the conditions for their co-existence.

Today India and China, which represent one-third of

the world's population, have become a trend of comparison. The situation is that China has emerged as one of the great power of Asia at this time. The unresolved border dispute between these two Asian superpowers is the core of mutual enmity. Both are also strategic rivals of each other, as both are suspicious of each other due to the confrontation of political thinking and strategic objectives. Recently, China has objected to the growing interest in the South China Sea and India's harsh attitude towards the Dalai Lama's issue has once again led to bitterness in the relations between the two countries. although there are many issues with China, such as not recognizing the Sikkim merger with India, the non-proliferation treaty between the two countries, the Dalai Lama's migration to India, his special and arms supply to Pakistan(Sino-Pakistan nexus), And in the context of India's permanent membership of the Security Council, the situation in South Asia in the current perspective, both countries will have to abandon their functionalist positions and take concrete initiative in terms of relations. However, both New Delhi and Beijing have taken the initiative to create and maintain a peaceful diplomatic environment. On this, economic liberalization and security of these two depends although little progress has been made towards resolving the issues dividing the two countries. Three issues mainly affect bilateral relations - border disputes, Tibet and trade.Two of these issues remain the same, but the third is flourishing in favor of China. The bilateral trade of $ 23 billion in 2000 has increased more than 20 times. Today, bilateral trade between the two has crossed the $ 40 billion mark.

The bitter truth is that Beijing is not ready to explain the Line of Control. Doing so will reduce military pressure on India. As a result, India and China are the only neighbors in the world who are not divided by a mutually defined Line of Control, despite the continuous dialogue. The truth is that China is largely responsible for the failure of the two countries' longest negotiations in world history because they did not want to make the wrongly occupied possession of the fifth part of Jammu and Kashmir a matter of dialogue. Rather it is seeking a re-demarcation of its borders from India to include the Tawang Valley in its territory, which is a strategically important corridor. China is reluctant to follow the rule that what it has occupied cannot be questioned, but only the areas it claims can be negotiated.

It is important to note that in the last few years there have been more than 500 incursions by the Chinese army into the Indian border. There are mainly two reasons behind this obstinate attitude of Beijing. First, the emergence of economic and military power has prompted Beijing to adopt an aggressive foreign policy. Secondly, with the expansion of infrastructural facilities in Tibet.

When Narendra Modi became the Prime Minister of India in 2014, the whole country was seeing many possibilities for India in him. The people of the country also had high hopes for India's relationship with China and Pakistan. In the beginning Narendra Modi also made a lot of efforts towards improving relations with all his neighbors. In this episode, in September 2014, the Chinese President reached Ahmedabad at the invitation of Modi. The way Modi received him; it seemed that relations between the two countries would improve. During this visit, 12 agreements were signed including new route of Kailash Mansarovar Yatra and cooperation in Railways. In addition, the two countries signed agreements related to regional issues and China's industrial park. At the same time, about 1000 soldiers of the Chinese People's Liberation Army (PLA) entered the Chumar area of Jammu and Kashmir from the hill. India raised this issue in front of the Chinese President but did not let any discontent in the negotiations on its behalf. In the same year, President Xi Jinping met with Prime Minister Modi respectively on the sidelines of the 6th BRICS Summit and the Leaders' Meetings on East Asia Cooperation in Myanmar. In 2015, Indian Prime

Minister Modi visited China. In the same year, President Xi Jinping met with Prime Minister Modi respectively on the sidelines of the 7th BRICS Summit in Ufa and the Leaders' Meetings on East Asia Cooperation in Malaysia. China decided to open the Nathu La Pass to Indian official pilgrims to Xizang. India celebrated the India Tourism Year in China. In 2016, Indian President Mukherjee visited China. Prime Minister Modi visited China to attend the G20 Summit in Hangzhou and met with President Xi Jinping on the sidelines. President Xi Jinping visited India to participate in the 8th BRICS Summit in Goa and met with Prime Minister Modi on the sidelines. China celebrated China Tourism Year in India. In 2017, President Xi Jinping met with Prime Minister Modi on the sidelines of the SCO Summit in Astana. Prime Minister Modi visited China to attend the 9th BRICS Summit.[9]

On June 18, 2017, tensions between the two countries started once again over the border dispute over Doklam and it lasted for about 73 days. It is important to note that the point joining India-Bhutan and China is called Doklam in India, 'Dok La' in Bhutan and 'Doklank' in China. Doklam is a plateau between the Ha Valley in Bhutan, the former Sikkim district in India, and Yedong County, China.

Some part of Doklam is adjacent to the Indian border in Sikkim, where China wants to build a road. The Indian Army opposed the construction of the road. The concern of India is that if this road is built, then the reach of China on this area like 'hen's neck' will be increased by 20 km wide link connecting the north eastern states of our country. At the same time, China reiterated its sovereignty and said that they have built the road in their area. Along with this he accused the Indian Army of "encroachment". The impact of this dispute was that China stopped Hindu pilgrims going from India to Kailash to go to Mansarovar Yatra. However, China later allowed 56 Hindu pilgrims to go ahead for the Mansarovar Yatra via Himachal Pradesh. The dispute eventually ended after India and China had a lot of tension over Doklam for about two months there is billions of dollars of trade between China and India. In 2014 China invested 116 billion dollars in India which increased to 160 billion dollars in 2014. Bilateral trade between India and China stood at around $ 88 billion in 2018-19. It is important to note that for the first time India succeeded in reducing the trade deficit with China by $ 10 billion.

The rapid expansion of India-China bilateral trade since the beginning of this century propelled China to emerge as our largest goods trading partner by 2008, a position which China continues to hold today. Since the beginning of the previous decade, bilateral trade between the two countries recorded exponential growth. In 2011, bilateral trade reached US$ 73.9 billion, before dipping to US$ 66 billion in 2012 and rebounding to US$ 71.65 in 2015. For last three years, the bilateral trade has registered robust two-digit growth. For the year 2018, bilateral trade increased by 13.34 % year-on-year to reach US$ 95.7 billion, with India's exports rebounding to US$ 18.83 billion registering positive growth of 15.21 % year-on-year after 3 years' continuous decline and growth of 39.11% in 2017. In 2018 India's imports from China grew by 12.89% to US$ 76.87 billion while the trade deficit widened to $ 58.04 billion. Trade figures for the past few years are as under[10].

Year	India's Export to China	India's Import from China	Trade Imbalance	Total Trade
2014	16.41	54.24	37.83	70.65
2015	13.39	58.26	44.87	71.65
2016	11.75	59.43	47.68	71.18
2017	16.34	68.1	51.76	84.44
2018	18.83	76.87	58.04	95.7
2019 Jan-Nov	16.32	68	51.68	84.32

Our trade deficit with China has been rising from the beginning of this century and was around US $48.66 billion in the year 2019-20. It has become a major sticking point in the bilateral relations. India imports 5 times what it exports for China. A big 'dependency syndrome' from China has been developed. India has been a particular victim of Chinese mercantilism. Opaque Chinese authorities permit imports of few Indian goods and services that have otherwise been globally competitive,thus perpetuating an exploitative, colonial-style trade relationship with India. For the past several years, the growing trade deficit had become a major challenge for India by continuously manipulating China.[11]

Consequent to the Doklam stand off in 2017 which lasted for 73 days, there have been two informal summits between Prime Minister Modi and President Xi Jinping at Wuhan in 2018 and at Mamallapuram in 2019.It was decided (at Mamallapuram) that the year 2020 would mark the 70th anniversary of the establishment of India-China diplomatic relations and the two countries would be organising 70 activities during 2020 to emphasise the historical connection between the two civilisations.[12]

On 10 May 2020, Chinese and Indian troops clashed in Nathu La, Sikkim, leaving 11 soldiers injured.[13] Following the skirmishes in Sikkim, tensions between the two countries grew in Ladakh (Galwan Valley)with a buildup of troops at multiple locations.[14] 20 Indian and few PLA soldiers were reportedly brutally killed in action on the night of 15/16 June.[15] Following the deaths, Prime Minister Modi addressed the nation about the incident, saying that "the sacrifice made by our soldiers will not go in vain", while the Indian foreign minister told the Chinese foreign minister that Chinese actions in Galwan were "pre-meditated".[16] The Chinese foreign minister said that both sides were trying to de-escalate the situation. Following the Galwan Valley clash on 15 June 2020, there were renewed calls across India to boycott Chinese goods, however, numerous Indian government officials said that border tensions would have little impact on trade.[17] The Chinese Minister of Defense Wei Fenghe and Indian Minister of Defense Rajnath Singh anticipated meeting at the Russian Victory Day Parade in Moscow on 23 June in order to discuss a way forward, but ultimately decided to cancel the bilateral meeting. As of 24 June, the highest level of bilateral discussion regarding the LAC tension has been between Corps-level military commanders.[18] On 29 June, the Indian government banned 59 widely-used Chinese mobile phone and desktop applications in response to rising tensions and escalating diplomatic dispute between the two nations.[19] Obviously, China has unilaterally changed the rules of the game. It is quite apparent that a new narrative is shaping up as far as Sino-Indian relations are concerned.

In the current Covid-19 pandemic spread and destruction of world global pace and order scenario the world has got divided into a pre-covid world and post-covid world but the one thing that remains unaltered is the harsh expansionist policy of China whose ethics pose a constant threat onto the global world.

China, as known to the world is a power of expansion. Over the last four thousand years Chinese expansion policy has been a central feature of the history of East Asia. Even today China with the rise of military, technology and economical power also pushes for expansion of its influence and power onto this world. China claims that the South China Sea has been it's territory since the ancient times and its worsening continuous disputes with India which is also known as the 'Pivot of Asia'. India and China being the more dominant and influensive countries of Asia have their own strategic ambitions to play a critical role in the emerging political, economic and strategic framework of Asia. It was always observed that China was reluctant to accept India's importance when the world was talking about rising of India. The current Ladakh dispute, doklam dispute, domination over Nepal, domination on World Health Organisation, denial of observation of Wuhan virology, forgery on medical supplies, claim on Taiwan and denial for accepting the decision of the International Court, BRI Project, 'String of Pearls' policy, Beggar-thy-neighbour policy, etc proves the self-centred intentions of these Chinese expansionism theory which is posing a worldwide threat to the Asian peace and security.

We misread the Chinese intentions in the events leading to 1962 and we have misread them again in 2020. Let us not do it again for the third time because that would be inexcusable.China, through CPEC projects hopes to become a third party in the Kashmir dispute between India and Pakistan. The latest development of the commencement of construction of Diamer-Basha Dam on the river Indus in Gilgit-Baltistan under CPEC is a serious development which poses a direct challenge to India's core interests. The Central Sector (Himachal Pradesh and Uttarakhand) requires urgent attention as that can also become a flash point. China claims approximately 2,000 square km of the territory in the Central Sector and that is under Indian control. We need to improve our infrastructure and defensive posture in the Central Sector so that China cannot create a Ladakh like.

India, has the support of majority of nations across globe today. It is no small deal having seanetors of USA back us up on the border dispute. India is also a QUAD member. On a worldwide scale,pacing towards an' Aatmnirbhar Bharat' India holds a very powerful and strong position as a nation. Scaling LAC TO LOC** India stands capable of defending itself. There is a flurry of anti-Chinese feeling amongst the nations of the world for its handling of the coronavirus and its aggressive behaviour in the South China Sea. The challenge for our political and military leadership strongis to turn this to our advantage in Tibet and elsewhere.

**Quoting P.M. Modi ji's Independence Day speech(15 August 2020)

To strengthen its ambition to become a global power, India needs to develop a military capability that extends beyond its territory. However, its navy has already made its mark far and wide. China is increasing strategic pressure on our country through three different routes. Given that China is not willing to maintain the status quo in the region in terms of agreement, India needs to adopt a more realistic, renewed, aggressive,and effective approach for its National interest.

References

1. Backus, Maria (September 2002). Ancient China. Lorenz Educational Press, 2002.
2. Janin, Hunt (January 1999). The India-China opium trade in the nineteenth century. McFarland, 1999.
3. Williams, Barbara (2005). World War Two. Twenty-First Century Books, 2004.
4. Ibid.
5. Joshi, Manoj (2017), Doklam: To start at the very beginning, Observer Research Foundation, archived from the original on 20 December 2017, retrieved 7 February 2018
6. Lancaster, John (12 April 2005). "India, China Hoping to 'Reshape the World Order' Together". The Washington Post. Archived from the original on 9 February 2011.
7. Laskar, Rejaul (December 2013). "Promoting National Interest through Diplomacy". Extraordinary and Plenipotentiary Diplomatist. **1** (9): 60.

   *-In the meeting with Mr. Rajiv Gandhi, the then chairman of China's central military commission Deng Xiaoping remarked-"Let us forget the unpleasant phase in our past relations and do everything with an eye on the future"
8. *thewire.in>security>india-china-xi-jinping-lac-border-modi-1962-war*, P.J.S. Sandhu(It is time to accept how badly India misread Chinese intensions in 1962-2020), 21 July 2020

9. *www.thehindu.com>brandhub>article31219737,* 70 years of diplomatic relations between China and India(1950-2020)'. (sponsored content),March 31, 2020

10. *https://www.eoibeijing.gov.in/economic-and-trade-relation.php.* (Embassy of India),India-China trade and economic relation.

11. Swagata Ganguly, 'The China Syndrome', The Times of India, Friday 19 June 2020, page 10.

12. *thewire.in>security>india-china-xi-jinping-lac-border-modi-1962-war,* P.J.S. Sandhu(It is time to accept how badly India misread Chinese intensions in 1962-2020). 21 july 2020

13. Janjua, Haroon (10 May 2020). *"Chinese and Indian troops injured in border brawl". The Times. Archived* from the original on 12 May 2020. Retrieved 12 May 2020.

14. Sushant Singh, *Chinese intrusions at 3 places in Ladakh, Army chief takes stock,* The Indian Express, 24 May 2020.

15. Pubby, Manu (17 June 2020). *"Over 20 soldiers, including Commanding Officer killed at Galwan border clash with China"*. The Economic Times. Retrieved 17 June 2020.

16. Laskar, Rezaul H; Singh, Rahul; Patranobis, Sutirtho (18 June 2020). "India warns China of serious impact on ties, Modi talks of 'befitting' reply". Hindustan Times. Retrieved 18 June 2020.

17. Suneja, Kirtika; Agarwal, Surabhi (17 June 2020). "Is This Hindi-Chini Bye Bye on Trade Front? Maybe Not: No immediate impact likely on business relations, say govt officials"(print version). The Economic Times.

18. *"India denies Chinese media report of meeting between Rajnath Singh and his counterpart Wei Fenghe". Zee News. 24 June 2020.* Retrieved 24 June 2020.

19. Tik Tok ban in India: Centre bans 59 mobile apps including Tik Tok, UC Browser, others". The Times of India. 29 June 2020. Retrieved 29 June 2020.

11

China's Nuclear Positioning: An Analytical Study

Dr. Mohammad Samir Hussain*
Dr. Janatun Begum**

Introduction

Chinese nuclear development has placed China among world class military superpowers, and has made it capable of delivering multiple large nuclear weapons to almost any location in the world. The direct threat from Chinese nuclear weapons depends largely on a country's relationship with China, as well as China's perception of military risk from a given state. But the greatest threat to the world emanates from the Chinese program of years of irresponsible nuclear proliferation that have armed dangerous states like Iran, North Korea, Pakistan, and others.[1]

In the 1950's, the Chinese government under Chairman

* Post Doctoral Fellow, Department of Defence Studies, Meerut College, Meerut.

** Lecturer, Department of Geography, Manipur College, Manipur

Mao chose to "Lean to one Side"– towards the Soviet Union, a friendly Communist government. Along with the United States' decision to declare the exiled Guomindang (GMD or KMT) in Taipei the legitimate government of all of China, the "Lean" decision caused a great rift between the United States and China. This rift caused the two countries to take hostile positions towards each other, and in the context of the Cold War, use of military or nuclear force was a real and significant danger. Specifically, Mao Zedong was worried about nuclear blackmail from the United States over the Taiwan issue, and accepted assistance from the U.S.S.R. in developing a nuclear weapons program. The Soviet Union granted to China an experimental nuclear reactor, gas diffusion equipment, a cyclotron, and many advisors to help the Chinese develop their weapon program.[2] Even when the relationship between China and the Soviet Union cooled significantly, China continued its nuclear weapons program on its own, and, much to the surprise of the United States Intelligence Community was nuclear-capable by 1964. China's great push towards the bomb came to crescendo on October 16 at a desolate hill called Lop Nur. Atop a 102-meter tower, the Chinese detonated a U-235 implosion type device, codenamed "596," that yielded 22 kilotons. It was less than three years later that China tested its first thermonuclear device. On June 17th, 1967, the Chinese detonated a 3.3 Megaton Hydrogen bomb at 2960 meters in the air.[3] The 32 months between first nuclear and first thermonuclear tests is shorter than any other nation's thermonuclear lag.

Beyond 1967, China has further accelerated its nuclear weapons program. The Chinese military quickly developed long-range nuclear delivery systems, targeting systems, and larger bombs. Some of this impressive development has drawn dark accusations: the Cox Report, released in January 1999, accused the Chinese government of stealing design documents for thermonuclear weaponry, Multiple Independently

Targetable Re-entry Vehicle (MIRV) technology, and long-range missile technology. The Chinese called the accusations "groundless," and maintained that all nuclear technology was indigenously developed. The swift rise of China's nuclear program is impressive, and has brought about a large and advanced arsenal capable of great damage throughout most of the world.[4]

China's nuclear programme is US centric but its nuclear proliferation and modernisation of Nuclear Forces do have ramifications in South Asia. Similarly India's nuclear programme is more driven by China's capabilities than of Pakistan. All efforts by India on nuclear front is to create an effective credible deterrence against nuclear blackmail. It is a common perception that Indo-Pak nuclear deterrence is far more prone to breakdown as compared to the India-China nuclear equation. The latter is believed to enjoy a greater level of stability. This assumption arises from four prevailing realities. Firstly, despite the fact that China illegally occupies 48,000 sq km of Indian territory and lays claim to another 90,000 sq kms in Arunachal Pradesh and some other sectors, unlike Pakistan, Beijing does not resort to the open use of direct asymmetric warfare to fulfil its revisionist ambitions.[5]

Therefore, while Pakistan's nuclear strategy of offensive defence carries the possibility of deterrence breakdown as a result of border skirmishes escalating to a larger conflict due to underlying anger and frustration at the constant terrorism inflicted on Indian society and nation, the possibility of a similar development between India and China is far less, even though alleged incursions are also made by the Chinese along the Line of Actual Control (LAC) with alarming frequency. Secondly, India and China also have some nuclear doctrinal consonances that enhance deterrence stability. Like China, India too strives for minimum credible nuclear deterrence and has declared a 'retaliation only' policy that is premised on the capability to cause unacceptable damage with the help of survivable and reliable nuclear forces after the adversary's first use of nuclear weapons. Such a position, even if the declaratory pronouncements are not legal commitments, makes the nuclear doctrines of both countries stand apart from those of other NWS. Also, it makes their relationship more stable as it is deemed less prone to deterrence breakdown as a result of misperceptions or miscalculations in times of crisis. Any nuclear use would have to be a deliberately considered choice, which is largely assumed to be a non-option for rational state actors.

Thirdly, most Chinese writings, quite similar to those in India too, perceive nuclear weapons as a political tool of deterrence. Both countries claim a defensive role for their nuclear arsenal, projecting it as an effective instrument that would be used to safeguard their nation against possible nuclear coercion or blackmail through the use of the threat to impose a high cost on the aggressor, so that no gains appear worthwhile. Thus, both seek to exploit the political benefit of the nuclear weapon, albeit by suitably enhancing the military aspect of its nuclear capability.

Fourthly, China and India are focused on economic development and it is widely assumed that Beijing would not undertake revisionist activities that would distract it from this goal till such a time when it is able to secure a certain global pre-eminence for itself. India, in any case, has never expressed a desire to revise its territorial limits through military means.

However, notwithstanding these stabilizing elements, there are factors that also complicate the Indo-China relations. Firstly, China still does not officially recognize India as a nuclear weapon state and hence has refused to undertake any nuclear arms control or nuclear stability negotiations with New Delhi. Secondly, China's NFU is believed not to apply to territories that it claims as its own (which would include Aksai Chin and the state of Arunachal

Pradesh). Thirdly, Beijing is engaged in a process of strategic modernization. Though these developments are perceived to be in response to US moves towards deployment of ballistic missile defence (BMD) and other policies such as those of pre-emption and counter proliferation the up gradation of its nuclear capabilities do cause anxieties in India owing to lack of clarity about Chinese intentions.[6]

China's Strategic Culture

Chinese strategic culture has been nurtured and matured over an epoch. It was greatly influenced by the teachings of Confucius, Sun Tzu and Maoist views. In addition, Chinese experience at the hands of Western nations and Japan in the 18th century. China is general, and Chinese strategic culture more specifically, was deeply affected by its experiences with almost all imperialist powers through the 19th and 20th centuries. Since the 1950s, when it was engaged in direct military confrontation with the US in the Korean War, China has continued to face American hostility in the form of diplomatic isolation, economic sanctions and military pressure.

The dominant strategic culture of China has historically stressed the limited, political uses of coercive diplomacy, and has eschewed crusading and offensive wars. This pattern, it has been argued, characterized imperial China and has persisted into the People's Republic. The secondary literature pretty much accepts the notion that in Chinese strategic thought and practice the use of violence was a "last resort".[7] This reluctance to resort to force rested, it is argued, on a low estimation of the efficacy of violence which was inherent in the Confucian moral order, and led to the "pacifist bias of the Chinese tradition". Different authors put it different ways: a stress on psychological warfare over the use of weaponry and firepower; a stress on "gaining victory while keeping as much intact as possible both socially and materially rather than destroying who or whatever stands in the way"; an "anti-militarist bias";[8] an emphasis on humans or mind over weaponry and the use of non-violent stratagem and deception to overcome "bare strength"; an "aversion to violence in war"; the absence of a notion of ideologically based total war; the minimization of war and the corollary that wars which were not minimized were ethically unjust; a "systematic denial of belligerence"; a view that war is an "aberration"; and "strategy by stratagem" as opposed, presumably, to strategy involving the application of violence among other similar characterizations.[9] If there is one single concept that has influenced contemporary Chinese strategic behavior, it has been that of deception. The Maoist-Leninist view propagates violent class struggle, the Confucian-Mencian notion of 'not fighting and subduing the enemy' can produce peace and security. It is therefore argued that 'not fighting and subduing the enemy' is at the heart of the theory of deterrence 'with Chinese characteristics'.[10] The strategy involved is akin to mind over matter: 'attacking the mind is superior to attacking fortification.[11]

Another alleged element of Chinese strategic thought and behaviour is a stress on limited wars, that is, military behaviour constrained by well-defined spatial and temporal restrictions on violence. China has been relatively successful, it is argued, in using limited amounts of force, in co-ordination with diplomatic tools, to pursue clearly defined, limited political aims. Grand strategic behaviour in the post-1949 period has been characterized by defence at or only slightly beyond "the gates," a relative rather than zero-sum concept of victory, pacification and deterrence, a non-zero sum concept of conflict which reduces pressures to escalate, and an ability to preserve a strict hierarchy of political goals in the midst of conflict, among other traits.[12]

Another strand in Chinese strategic culture has been the shift towards minimum use of force if violence does become necessary. Offensive wars of annihilation have not been resorted to in Chinese history. This is linked to what is called 'limited war' in strategic thought. One can locate international use of force by China from 1950-79 in these board categories: to recover territories to which China lays claim (Sino-Indian war), to deter a perceived superpower attack (involvement in the Korean war), and to maintain regional balance of power (Sino-Vietnam border war in 1979). Most of these have been limited military engagements. In chapter 3 of Sun Tzu's *Art of War* on 'Planning Offensive', there are details of how energy (chi) constitutes a basis for the kingdom's forces (Li) and how extended operations or battles reduce military forces.[13] For instance, Mao's time, this principle was much in practice: China's civil war campaign at Pingjin lasted for 56 days; the Sino-Indian war 1962 lasted for 20 days, Huainan for 65 days and the Vietnam War in 1979 for 29 days.[14] After the Cold War, China's new leaders formally pronounced limited war as a war-fighting doctrine.

Yet again, it is Sun Tzu whose dictum of a short swift war dominates and is considered better than long campaigns. 'In war, then, let your great object be victory, not lengthy campaigns.' In fact, if the enemy can be defected even without fighting, it is considered supreme excellence: 'to fight and conquer in all your battles is not supreme excellence; supreme excellence consists in breaking the enemy's resistance without fighting. In fact, it has been clearly written that 'there is no instance of a country having benefited from prolonged warfare.'[15] The changing nature of the PLA and its transformation to a 'lean mean fighting machine' has connotations for a move towards what Sun Tzu had advised – short war.

Important element of China's strategic culture is that the armed forces are considered central in the society and in national security planning. Sun Tzu laid special emphasis on the military as another indicator of national power, a theme that continues in China's contemporary strategic culture. In the late 1970s, China initiated comprehensive reorganization (zhengbian), a process that is still going on. This reorganization was based on the principle, *Suojian bujun youqi shi bubing yuan's jiaang gongjum, haijun, jige tezhing bing budai* (reduce ground forces, particularly infantry personnel, strengthen air force, navy as well as special forces – nuclear, chemical and biological weapons).[16]

China's Nuclear Doctrine

The phenomenal rise of China in the 21st century has been the most debated issue in the world for the past few years. At the same time, not many are sure about the probable change in the Chinese behavior because of the newly acquired economic, military and technological might. Several Asian and other countries are closely monitoring the Chinese rise and still assessing the short and long term implications on their national security interests. China's growing economic and military power has led to concerns over how it would readjust its politics and reshape the existing rules and regulations according to its newly acquired status.[17] Despite its repeated claims of peaceful rise, China's nuclear and missile modernization is a matter of concern. China's ongoing military modernization and the growing assertiveness of its military in the Indian and the Pacific Ocean region could create security dilemmas for many Asian countries.

Since the Lop Nur test in 1964, when China became a declared nuclear power, it has never publicly discussed its nuclear doctrine. As Johnston put it, 'for about 30 years after China exploded its first nuclear weapon there was no coherent, publicly articulated nuclear doctrine.[18] The only openly stated position then was that these weapons were to prevent blackmail and coercion by the other nuclear powers, principally, the US and then the Soviet Union. China's nuclear strategy has never been as explicitly stated as those of some other countries. But it is believed that China has the following five objectives for its nuclear strategy: (i) secure super power status; (ii) preclude the possibility of intrusive diplomacy through nuclear coercion; (iii) deter other nuclear regimes (such as breakaway states from the former Soviet Union); (iv) retain a trump card for the eventually that Japan may rescind its current pacifist policies for a military option; and (v) maintain political and moral ascendancy over its regional rivals (such as India). The small number of nuclear weapons in the Chinese military limits the ability to have a counter – force strategy. Consequently, the Chinese have adopted a strategy of minimum deterrence.

Defence White Paper published in 2006 by Beijing took the unprecedented step of discussing China's nuclear strategy in a document intended for public consumption.[19] That document discussed the role of the PLA Navy in conducting "nuclear counterattacks" and the importance of the Second Artillery Force as a strategic deterrent, and described China's approach to nuclear weapons in the following terms:

China's nuclear strategy is subject to the state's nuclear policy and military strategy. Its fundamental goal is to deter other countries from using or threatening to use nuclear weapons against China. China remains firmly committed to the policy of no first use of nuclear weapons at any time and under any circumstances. It unconditionally undertakes not to use or threaten to use nuclear weapons against non-nuclear-weapon states or nuclear-weapon-free zones, and stands for the comprehensive prohibition and complete elimination of nuclear weapons. China upholds the principles of counterattack in self-defense and limited development of nuclear weapons, and aims at building a lean and effective nuclear force capable of meeting national security needs. It endeavours to ensure the security and reliability of its nuclear weapons and maintains a credible nuclear deterrent force. China's nuclear force is under the direct command of the Central Military Commission (CMC). China exercises great restraint in developing its nuclear force. It has never entered into and will never enter into a nuclear arms race with any other country.[20]

Absent definitive statements from the PLA or its political masters, the shape of Beijing's nuclear strategy remained obscure. Some understanding may be gleaned from articles penned (obviously, with official sanction) by senior military leaders and thinkers. Wang Zhongchun, both a Senior Colonel and a Professor at the PLA's National Defence University (as well as a former visiting scholar at the US Army's Strategic Studies Institute), laid out the strategic function of China's nuclear forces in a recent edition of *China Security*, arguing that "China's nuclear weapons play multiple strategic roles":

> First, nuclear weapons hold up China's power status and its position as one of the five permanent members of the United Nations. Second, as a retaliatory strategic force, nuclear weapons are an indispensable deterrent to those nuclear states that put China on their 'nuclear strike lists'. Finally, nuclear weapons, as 'an assassin's mace', can be used at a time when China's core national security and development interests are fundamentally undermined.[21]

In 2010 Retired Peoples' Liberation Army Major General XU Guangyu in People's Daily argued that:

> China wanted a minimal nuclear deterrent and would avoid any arms race. China resolutely adheres to a defensive nuclear strategy, and has always adhered to a policy that it will never be the first to use nuclear weapons at any time and under any circumstances. The most basic feature of China's nuclear strategy, in a nutshell, is to be a deterrent but present no threat. China must have a nuclear force that is real, reliable, effective, and keeps up with the times. That force includes a second-strike capability so China can retaliate if it comes under nuclear attack. This force is able, should a foe launch an

> initial nuclear strike, to really possess, and to convince the other side that it faces, an intolerable second-strike nuclear capability, thereby deterring an enemy from using nuclear weapons against us. It must make them grasp, without the least ambiguity, that we possess a deterrent. International experience shows the most effective second-strike capability is submarines.[22]

Minimum Credible Deterrence

China has officially declared minimum deterrence as its nuclear strategy. The Chinese understanding and practice of the strategy of minimum deterrence is, nevertheless, dynamic. Its features are continuously adjusted to meet the changing strategic environment and threats at regional and global levels.[23] The minimum deterrence broadly refers to the China's interactions at the global level vis-à-vis other NWS.

In keeping with the Chinese strategic culture of minimalism and ambiguity, Mao directed his country to steer clear of an excessive build-up of nuclear warheads in favour of an arsenal that would be just enough to inflict unacceptable damage. It was Mao's dictum to "build a few, keep the number small, make the quality high" and he is also cited to have stated, "Six are enough"[24]. In Western literature, this came to be described as minimum nuclear deterrence. This was premised on the use of nuclear weapon as a political tool of deterrence, which clearly obviated the need for nuclear superiority, or even parity. Consequently, China has aimed for a capability that would be sufficient to deter threats of nuclear use against itself. Mao's rationale for such a doctrine was as much a result of circumstantial resource constraints of funds and fissile material, as the astute understanding that Washington would never risk a nuclear exchange with China. Rather, Beijing found greater wisdom in setting an "example of moderation and prudence on the moral high ground, and seemingly proved its theory that small defensively oriented arsenals at once provided deterrence, reassurance and stability".[25] Mutual vulnerability was believed to be good enough and China never strove for MAD. In fact, even in 1969, at the time of the Ussuri river conflict with the USSR – the first time ever that two neighbouring nuclear armed states engaged in armed conflict, and amid reports that the Soviets may be preparing for a disarming first strike against Chinese nuclear assets – Marshal Nie Rongzhen, in a report to the Central Committee concluded, "It is not an easy matter to use a nuclear weapon. When a country uses nuclear weapons to threaten another country, it places itself under the threat of the other country's nuclear weapons..."[26] The emphasis, therefore, was on building high-yield nuclear weapons for counter value targeting, so that destruction was assured even without accurate delivery systems. Consequently, the Chinese nuclear arsenal was never swayed by the Superpower logic of large nuclear stockpiles. It sought rather an assured counter strike capability against value targets as a powerful deterrent because the Chinese measure of the effectiveness of its arsenal was the adversary's psychological fear of suffering retaliation, rather than a calculation based on its own force structure. It was truly a case of achieving deterrence through punishment rather than through any pretension of being able to fight a nuclear war in which China could deny victory to the adversary.[27]

However, it was only to be expected that with economic development and the concomitant easing of purse strings, as also techno-scientific advancements and change in threat perceptions and core interests, the nature of China's nuclear deterrent too would alter. China's development or acquisition of advanced strategic capabilities is driven as much by the new threats (such as the development and deployment of BMD by the US and its export to Taiwan), as by the logical progression of its economic prowess and techno-scientific expertise. Some Western experts on China describe this as graduation from minimum to limited nuclear deterrence. The essential difference lies in the fact that while minimum only required China to maintain a credible counter strike capability based on survivable nuclear forces, limited deterrence entails the possession of more sophisticated nuclear forces capable of controlling escalation during a conflict and bringing about intra-war deterrence.[28] This envisages a flexible nuclear response, including counterforce targeting, instead of basing deterrence on only counter-value punitive strikes. The emphasis, therefore, shifts to acquisition of "limited warfighting capabilities, improved command and control and early warning systems, smaller, survivable, mobile, more accurate and diverse cruise and ballistic missile nuclear delivery systems, possible abandonment of the NFU policy, and missile defence".[29] Some other analysts, however, such as Evan S Medeiros, have described these moves as being driven by "sufficiency and effectiveness". It should be sufficient in size to resist enemy efforts to coerce China by threatening retaliation, and in case that fails, sufficient enough to survive an enemy's initial strike and effective enough to execute counter-attack and re-attack operations to inflict unacceptable damage, and to penetrate whatever defenses the enemy may employ.[30]

The strategy of minimum deterrence is currently under intense debate in China, with some critics within the defence establishment seeing the future as demanding a more flexible approach. This has given rise to speculation on whether China has moved from minimum deterrence to limited deterrence, and whether there is a shift from countervalue targeting to counterforce targeting. A shift from minimum to limited deterrence would mean that China is developing warfighting capability. Some analysts argue that China is now pursuing a three-pronged approach: (i) credible minimal deterrent against the United States and Russia; (ii) limited deterrence around its periphery where local conflict is conceivable; and (iii) offensively configured counterforce strategy, with even a pre-emptive hypothesis. The second and third approaches are of direct significance to Indian security.[31]

There is a remarkable difference between the Chinese nuclear posture of the 1980s and now. While earlier, nuclear deterrence was solely based on ambiguity and secrecy in numbers and capability (indicating greater reliance on existential deterrence), it is now more credibly derived from mobility, invulnerability and penetrability of nuclear forces. This change is the result of both China's perception that is has been accommodated in the outside world, as well as an increase in the number, variety and quality of its nuclear forces.

Much of the debate revolves around whether China pursues either minimum deterrence or limited deterrence. Minimum deterrence refers to 'threatening the lowest level of damage necessary to prevent attack, with the fewest number of nuclear weapons possible'. Similarly, limited deterrence 'requires a limited war-fighting capability to inflict costly damage on the adversary at every rung on the escalation ladder, thus denying the enemy victory in a nuclear war'. Some hint of the outline of Beijing's philosophy vis-à-vis the question of minimal vs. limited deterrence may be inferred from the 'Five Musts' articulated by Jiang Zemin at the Central Military Commission's conference in July 2000. Jiang's 'Five Musts' point clearly in the direction of a policy of limited deterrence.[32] These were expressed as follows:

- China must own strategic nuclear weapons of a definite quality and quantity in order to ensure national security;
- China must guarantee the safety of strategic nuclear bases and prevent against the loss of combat effectiveness from attacks and destruction by hostile countries;
- China must ensure that its strategic nuclear weapons are at a high degree of war preparedness;

- When an aggressor launches a nuclear attack against China, China must be able to launch nuclear counterattack and nuclear re-attack against the aggressor;
- China must pay attention to the global situation of strategic balance and stability and, when there are changes in the situation, adjust its strategic nuclear weapon development strategy in a timely manner.

Opacity

Opaqueness has become the hallmark of Chinese Nuclear doctrine. In the years to come, China's nuclear doctrine, despite its on-going evolution, will probably remain pivoted on ambiguity by design.[33] Another alternative for maintaining the credibility of a nuclear retaliatory force is constructive ambiguity – the approach adopted by Israel since it became an unacknowledged NWS at some point shortly after China did. While the PRC is an openly-acknowledged NWS, it has adopted some of the same principles as Israel with respect to its nuclear forces, maintaining a high degree of secrecy and operational security, and refusing to confirm or deny details reported in open source literature. Imprecise knowledge about the size, shape and status of China's strategic forces suggests that, in time of war, an adversary contemplating a disarming first strike would never be able to be certain that he had located all of China's weapons. Further ambiguity derives from the variety of launch mechanisms China has adopted – fixed launch platforms, silo-based launchers, and road-mobile transport-erector-launcher (TEL) systems, in addition to SLBMs and aircraft-delivered cruise missiles and gravity bombs (for theatre missions), which taken altogether make it more difficult for a potential adversary to ensure that he has found and destroyed all potential threats. Some analysts have suggested that Beijing is comfortable with "the ambiguity surrounding the survivability of its nuclear forces".[34]

No-First Use (NFU) Policy

China is only NWS to have advocated a no-first use policy of nuclear weapons. China's NFU pledge originates in the statement issued by Beijing on the occasion of its first nuclear test on 16 October 1964: "The Chinese government hereby solemnly declares that China will never at any time or under any circumstances be the first to use nuclear weapons."[35] In the 1960s, 70s and 80s, as a developing country, China used to support the views of other third-world countries by opposing the nuclear wepons development by the western countries. It also urged the other NWS to agree on an international treaty on the NFU policy. The latest defence white paper released by China mentions that:

> As a permanent member of the UN Security Council and a nuclear-weapon state signatory of the NPT, China has never evaded its obligations towards nuclear disarmament and pursues an open, transparent and responsible nuclear policy. It has adhered to the policy of no-first-use of nuclear weapons at any time and in any circumstances, and made the unequivocal commitment that under no circumstances will it use or threaten to use nuclear weapons against non-nuclear-weapon states or nuclear-weapon-free-zones. China has never deployed nuclear weapons in foreign territory and has always exercised the utmost restraint in the development of nuclear weapons, and has never participated in any form of nuclear arms race, nor will it ever do so. It will limit its nuclear capabilities to the minimum level required for national security[36].

However, there are indications to suggest that China has modified and diluted its NFU policy. It started its NFU pledge against all countries, but over the years it has been modified and as of now, it is directed towards NNWS Party to the NPT and nuclear weapons free zones. Thus, India and the other NWS have been excluded from this pledge. The revised posture, released by the Ministry of Foreign

Affairs in Beijing on 5 April 1995 and placed in the records of the Geneva-based Conference on Disarmament the following day, states that China's policy not to use or threaten to use nuclear weapons "naturally applies to non-nuclear-weapon states parties to the Treaty on the Non-Proliferation of Nuclear Weapons (NPT) or non-nuclear-weapon states that have undertaken any comparable internationally binding commitments not to manufacture or acquire nuclear explosive devices." The shift from an unconditional to a conditional NFU posture effectively left out only India, Israel and Pakistan. The policy change, however, could not be directed at close ally, Pakistan, or even Israel, with whom Beijing has collaborated in military-technology projects. The shift appeared aimed at sending a message to New Delhi.[37] Besides, there is criticism that the NFU lacks credibility as it is not verifiable and can be easily changed at a time of crisis.[38] According to this logic, when faced with an adverse situation or a crisis in which the strategic gains of breaking the NFU pledge are higher than abiding by it, China will have an incentive to break its promise. The NFU policy though tactically conditionally remains symbolic of its apparent promise of rising peacefully. The NFU posture compels China to maintain a strong survivable deterrent capability for retaliation.

On 16 April 2013, China's State Council published a White Paper titled The Diversified Employment of China's Armed Forces Page. This 2013 edition is an update on the 2011 White Paper. While there are several elements of continuity, there are also important differences. According to the White Paper, PLA Second Artillery Force (PLASAF), PLA's nuclear force capabilities of "strategic deterrence, nuclear counterattack and conventional precision strike are being steadily elevated". For the first time, the White Paper did not explicitly mention the "no first use" doctrine but it laid emphasis on strategic deterrence and counter attack.

Non-mention of the No First Use has led many observers to debate whether China is beginning to dilute its NFU commitment. This will need to be watched.[39]

Nuclear Proliferation

Over the years China has played proliferation card far and wide, supplying missiles or missile components to Iran, Iraq, Libya, North Korea, Saudi Arabia and Syria, and nuclear materials or technology to Algeria, Argentina, Brazil, Iran, Iraq, North Korea and South Africa. U.S. intelligence has called China the "most significant supplier" of WMD goods and technology. But all of China's other proliferation activity pales in comparison to its extensive and sustained transfers to Pakistan. The transfers have included nuclear-warhead blueprints, complete missiles and technologies for local production. It is evident that as long as Pakistan survives, China will use it to countervail India.

Three different theories have been put forth to explain China's proliferation conduct: (i) that it is on a learning curve, and that it is gradually becoming more responsible, as evidenced by its joining the nonproliferation regime; (ii) profit motives; and (iii) that it consciously plays the proliferation card for leverage and containment. While China certainly wants to present itself as a responsible state by signing international agreements, it often prefers not to meet its obligations under these agreements. While commercial motivations are no doubt important in Confucian thinking, China values its horizontal proliferation most as an indispensable component of balance-of-power politics. The objectives of its proliferation activities are threefold: (i) countervailing or gaining leverage on the United States, India and Japan; (ii) building client states; and (iii) obtaining advanced military technology in exchange. These objectives explain why China has constantly broken its non proliferation pledges to Washington since 1993.[40]

China's Nuclear Arsenal

Nuclear Warheads. Of the five legally recognized nuclear weapon states, only China appears to be expanding the size of its nuclear arsenal. Comparative holding of world's nuclear warheads is depicted in the table below. In 2012, China conducted a comprehensive series of missile trials consolidating its road-mobile, land-based and submarine-based nuclear deterrent.

Table 1: World Nuclear Forces, 2013

Country	Deployed warheads	Other warheads	Total inventory
USA	2150	5550	7700
Russia	1800	6700	8500
UK	160	65	225
France	290	10	300
China	-	250	250
India	-	90 - 110	90 - 110
Pakistan	-	100 - 120	100 - 120
Israel	-	80	80
North Korea	-	6 - 8	6 - 8
Total	**4400**	**12865**	**17270**
All estimates are approximate and are as of January 2013.			

Source: SIPRI Yearbook 2013.

Missile Forces. China is aware of the fact that ensuring the survivability of its nuclear forces is its utmost priority. The survivability of its strategic nuclear force is enhanced through greater mobility, including deployment of solid-fuelled and road-mobile intercontinental ballistic missiles (ICBMs) and nuclear submarines.[41] Chinese strategic forces are made up of a triad of land-based missiles, submarines-launched missiles and bombers. The modernization of its missile and submarine forces, in turn, strengthens China's overall conventional forces vis-à-vis US. The US Department of Defence (DoD) reports that since 2000, China has shifted from a largely vulnerable, strategic deterrent based on liquid fuelled ICBMs fired from fixed platforms, to a more survivable and flexible strategic force.[42] According to the US DoD's Military Power of the PRC 2007, "China is developing and testing missiles, forming additional missile units, upgrading qualitatively certain missile systems, and developing methods to counter ballistic missile defenses".[43]

An important modernization program concerns a third generation of solid propellant, mobile and land-based ICBMs. The Chinese land based missile inventory includes two varieties of ICBMs, namely DF-5A (CSS-4), a three-stage liquid-propellant missile with a range of 13,000 km and DF-31A (CSS-9), a three-stage, solid fuelled ICBM with a range of 11,200 km. The DF-31A is an improved version of DF-31 (three-stage, solid fuel and range 8000 km).[44] The DF-31A can carry a warhead of 1 MT with MIRV capability.[45] In addition, China is also believed to be developing a three-stage solid propellant DF-41 (CSS-X-10) ICBM with a range more than 12000 km.[46] Some reports claim that the missile is likely to be operational by 2015 and China would field about 50-100 DF-41s.[47]

The survivability of these forces is higher than its other strike forces which can be destroyed in a pre-emptive strike. According to the International Institute for Strategic Studies, (IISS) Military Balance 2010, the breakup of these missiles are DF-31 (12); DF-31 A (24), DF-5A (20) and DF-4 (10) making a total of 66. However, there was no mention of DF-41 ICBMs in the report. The mainstay of the Chinese IRBM inventory is the DF-21 which is a two-stage solid propellant road-mobile missile. Though the DF-21 deployment started in the late 1980s, the process gained momentum from 2005. The inventory also includes DF-3A (two stage CSS-2) which was inducted in 1971. The DF-3A is a liquid-propellant missile with a range of about 3000 km. China has deployed several hundreds of short-range ballistic missiles like DF-15 (CSS-6 or M-9) and DF-11 (CSS-7 or M-11) missiles.

Naval Forces. Building advanced sea-based strike as will anti-access capabilities is the primary objective of China's naval modernization. China's naval modernization effort, which began in the 1990s, encompasses a broad array of weapon acquisition programs, including programs for anti-ship ballistic missiles (ASBMs), anti-ship cruise missiles (ASCMs), land-attack cruise missiles (LACMs), surface-to-air missiles (SAM), manned aircraft, unmanned aircraft, submarines, destroyers and frigates, strike capability includes the Type 092 nuclear submarine that carries twelve single-warhead JL-1 SLBMs.[48] The Jin class 094 SSBN is an important milestone that contributes to the deterrent capability. According to the IISS' Military Balance 2010 China has two Jin-class submarines, each equipped with 12 JL-2 SLBMs, though the full-operational status is unknown. The report also mentions that two more Jin class submarines are under development. In 2008, the Federation of Atomic Scientist reported that the SSBN was deployed near the Hainan Island on the South China Sea. The report stated,

> "The Chinese navy has deployed a Jin-class (Type 094) ballistic missile submarine to a new base near Yulin on Hainan Island on the South China Sea, according to a satellite image obtained by FAS. The image shows the submarine moored at a pier close to a large sea-entrance to an underground facility."[49]

As part of showcasing its capabilities, the PLA Navy (PLAN) demonstrated in April 2009, during the 60th anniversary celebrations, the SSBNs for the first time. In order to build more such Type 094 SSBNs, it has modified its structure by reducing the number of carriage missiles to twelve rather than sixteen which is standard practice in other navies.[50] The reduced size adds more stealth to the submarine. In this way China can build more 094 to increase the probability that some can survive a pre-emptive strike. The exact number of submarines being built by China is not known though there was speculation that China would build six such SSBNs. According to a report from the Office of Naval Intelligence (ONI), China will build at least five 094 strategic nuclear submarines.[51] A Naval War College study on China's new SSBN program predicts a fleet of six 094 submarines.[52]

China test fired a long-range SLBM in June 2005 which is believed to be a JL-2, though PLA officials do not comment on that.[53] China's JL-2 SLBM has a range of 8000 km and can carry multiple independently targetable reentry vehicle (MIRV).[54] The missile was reportedly fired by a nuclear submarine off the coast of Qingdao and landed in a Chinese desert. It may be concluded that the JL-2 is still under development. The new SSBN and SLBM capabilities marks a revolution in Chinese nuclear capability since it will provide China, for the first time, with a truly robust deterrence with diffused capabilities.

Anti-Ship Ballistic Missile Programme (ASBM). The US Department of defence believes that china is developing and testing anti-ship ballistic missile equipped with maneuverable reentry vehicles designed to hit moving ships at sea.

Ballistic Missile Defence Capability. For many years, China along with Russia was a staunch opponent of the US ballistic missile defence systems. Both viewed the US ballistic missile defence system as undermining their nuclear deterrence. China is also wary of US sale of weapons to

Taiwan including the PAC-3 air defence missiles. Thus, the Chinese anti-satellite test of January 11, 2007 came as a shock to many countries. It successfully intercepted and destroyed an aging weather satellite, Fengyun-1C at a height of 850 km in the lo-earth orbit using a two-stage intermediate-range ballistic missile (SC-19) a derivative of DF-21 MRBM. The test was criticized by many countries and concerns were expressed on the large debris created by this test. There were reports suggesting that the PLA had earlier tried the same test at a North Western desert in March 2006.[55]

Table 2: China's Nuclear Weapon Delivery Systems

Type	NATO Designation	No	Year Deployed	Range (kms)	Warheads X Yield (kt)	Warheads
Land Based Missiles						
DF-3A	CSS-2	17	1971	3,100	1 x 3,300	17
DF-4	CSS-3	17	1980	5,400	1 x 3,300	17
DF-5A	CSS-4	20	1981	13,000+	1 x 4,000-5,000	20
DF-21	CSS-5	55	1991	2,100	1 x 200-300?	55
DF-31	?	~6	2008	7,200+	1 x 200-300?	~6
DF-31A	?	~6	2008	11,200+	1 x 200-300?	~6
Submarine-Launched Ballistic Missiles						
JL-1*	CSS-NX-	30	1986	1,000+	1 x 200-300	0
JL-2	CSS-NX-	40	2009-10?	7,200+	1 x 200-300?	0
Aircraft**						
Hong-6	B-6	20	1965	3,100	1 x bomb	~20
					DH-10	~15

Qian-5 And others	Q-5	?	1972-?	-	1 x bomb	~20

* The JL-1 was never fully operational.

** Figures are for nuclear-configured aircraft only. Hundreds of aircraft are deployed in non-nuclear versions. Aircraft range is equivalent to combat radius; assumes a small stockpile of nuclear bombs with yields between 10 kilotons and 3 megatons.*** About 65 additional warheads may be in storage.

Source: Robert S. Norris and Hans M. Kristensen (2010) "Chinese Nuclear Forces", 2010, Bulletin of the Atomic Scientist 66(6): 134"141. DOI:10.1177/0096340210387046

Map: China's Missile Ranges

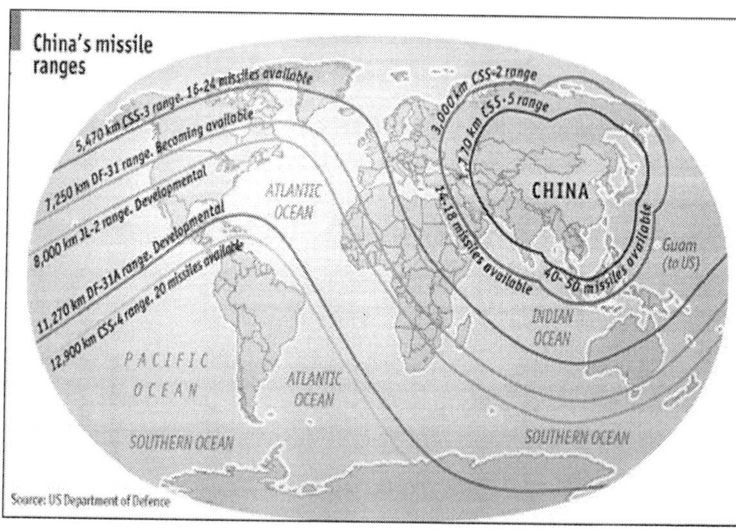

Source: US Department of Defence, (*http://www.defence.pk/forums/chinese-defence/84215-chinese-missiles-news-discussions.html*).

Exactly after three years, China announced that it had conducted a ground-based midcourse missile interception technology from within its territory. Without giving much details of the test, China said that the test has achieved the expected objective and that the test was defensive in nature and not targeted at any country. Chinese experts were quoted to have defended the test by stating that China has always followed a defensive strategy and that the present test also reinforces the strategy.[56] Without providing details on the purpose of the test and employed missiles (both target and interceptor), China allowed others to guess the capability and purpose of the test. It was well anticipated that China will embark on building ballistic missile defence capabilities. Experts are debating whether the missile defense system tested by China was the HQ-9 surface-to-air missile system or other.[57] In any case, the development of the Chinese ballistic missile defence system is likely to impinge negatively on the stability in the region and could trigger a potential arms race.

Maximization of Aero-Space Dominance. China is also known to be modernizing its air force with fourth-generation fighters, which carry beyond visual range (BVR) missiles. The PLA Air Force (PLAAF) operates numerous airborne early warning and control (AEW&C) and electronic warfare (EW) aircraft. China operates atleast a dozen AEW&C aircraft, many strike aircraft are now equipped with precision-guided munitions (PGMs). China's EW capabilities have improved substantially too[58]. There has been a marked shift in Chin's thinking on air power which reflected in its two white papers. The 2004 national defense white paper clearly stipulates that the role of Air power is no more that of auxiliary force to the ground and missile forces but has a clear mandate for offensive operations. The thinking has clearly evolved further nd the 2008 national defense white paper stipulates that the PLAAF have clear mission of "strategic projection". Though the word 'power' is missing in strategic projection it could be anybody's guess as to PLAFF has a clear role in power projection and has developed certain capabilities to execute long-range precision strikes and strategic projection operations.[59]

J-20 Stealth Aircraft. Almost after a year of the missile interception test and coinciding with the visit of the US Defence Secretary, Robert Gates to Beijing, China flight-tested its new stealth fighter J-20 in January 2011 from an airfield in the city of Chengdu. The fighter flew for abour 15 minutes. Earlier, the flight underwent high-speed taxing tests. The test of the stealth fighter is being seen as the growing interest of China in military modernization.

Unmanned Space Shuttle. Closely following on the heels of the US, unconfirmed reports in January 2011 suggested that China successfully conducted a flight-test of a prototype aircraft that can fly through the atmospheric layer.[60] The Ming Pao daily and the Zhongguo Pinglun, a new website, posted an article headlined that "China succeeds in spacecraft test in tandem with US X37B Orbital Test Vehicle". However, there was no official confirmation from Chinese authorities on the test.

Trends in Chinese Modernisation

Towards the end of 1990s, the US Department of Defence undertook an assessment of the ability of some countries to produce advanced equipment such as command, control, communications, computers, intelligence, information (C4I2) systems; high-performance computing; intelligent systems; signal processing: transmission system; opto-electronics, etc. It rated countries' capabilities on a scale of zero to four. While the US was at four, China received one, indicating a minimum level of proficiency.[61] Indeed, china is well aware of its limitations in these spheres, as well as of their criticality in wars of the future. The focus, therefore, is on "informationization" in its WPND 2004,

2006 and 2009. Evidently, the White Papers indicate an intelligent prioritisation of capability development to enhance Chinese security and exploit American vulnerabilities. Some of the specific efforts being undertaken by China to enhance the credibility of its nuclear deterrence are highlighted in the following paragraphs: - Nuclear deterrence in second tier nuclear weapon states

(a) **Increase in Size of Nuclear Arsenal.** The most obvious response to BMD would be to increase the number of warheads and strategic missiles to saturate and defeat the missile defence. Estimate of the numbers of its nuclear warheads vary from 200 to 450. For instance, the *Bulletin of Atomic Scientist* derives numbers on the basis of delivery vehicles to calculate that China deploys approximately 176 warheads (about 121 on land-based missiles, none yet on SLBNs and 55 on nuclear capable aircraft). Along with some additional warheads in storage, the total conservatively placed at 240.[62] Some others, though, report about 300 strategic and 150 tactical nuclear weapons. Meanwhile, a leaked Defence Intelligence Agency (DIA) estimate from 1999 stated that China's total nuclear inventory would increase to 358-464 warheads by 2020.[63] Another source reveals plans to deploy 500 nuclear warheads by 2015, with 300 on MIRVed and the rest on SLBMs.[64] US officialdom also predicts an increase of ICBMs from the present about 20 to 75-100 by 2015, some of which would have multiple warheads.[65] In fact, according to the National resource Defence Council estimates, China should have enough fissile material stockpiles to double or even treble its nuclear warheads and even the RAND Corporation finds it feasible for the warheads to increase to anything between 600-1,500.

(b) **Improvements in Mobility and Survivability of delivery Systems.** Concealment to enhance survivability was always central to Chinese nuclear deterrence. In order to enhance the survivability, accuracy and mobility of its strategic forces, China has been engaged in transcending to more solid fuelled, rail and road mobile missiles. China has begun deploying a new generation of solid fuelled mobile missiles, the DF-21A which is credited to have global positioning system (GPS) or radar-based terminal guidance for greater accuracy. Meanwhile, still development are the DF-31 and DF-31A, ICBMs that will form the core of its future strategic land-based missile force. The DF-31, flight tested since 1999, is likely to be single warhead missile, but equipped with decoy warheads and other counter-measures to penetrate US BMD. The sea leg of the Chinese nuclear triad would credibly rest on Julang (JL-2), a second generation SLBM that would be deployed on an indigenous Type 094 submarine that is expected to become operational by the end of this decade. One Xia class SSBN with 12 JL-1 missiles of 2,150 km range has been operational since 1988. Meanwhile, 100 H-6 bombers capable of carrying three bombs over 3,100 km and about 30 Q-5 aircraft that could carry one bomb over 400 km have constituted the third leg of the Chinese triad.

(c) **Development of MIRV Technology**. A report in December 2002 announced the test of DF-21 medium range ballistic missile (MRBM) with multiple warheads, a capability necessary to enhance China's nuclear deterrence against BMD.[66]

(d) **Rapid Enhancement of Space-Based Capabilities.** It is evident that China is modernising its space-based capabilities to directly attack enemy's space-based infrastructure with anti-satellite (ASAT) weapons, and to attack the enemy's ground-based radars or other electronic components of the command, control, communications, computers, intelligence, surveillance, reconnaissance (C4ISR) structure. Beijing has determined that a robust ASAT capability could counter the United States by disabling the "complex" exposed network of command, control, communications, and computer-based systems that provide intelligence [and] reconnaissance" to American Forces.[67] In fact, it may not be a pure coincidence that the technical parameters of China's January 11, 2007 ASAT test were akin to a ballistic missile intercept. The use of a phased array radar to guide a kinetic-kill vehicle toward a target (an ageing weather satellite) travelling at 7.2 km a second, or as fast as an ICBM would be when entering the earth's atmosphere was obviously conducted to send a message. China has also developed high altitude electro-magnetic pulse (EPM) with a nuclear device capable of exploding at 40 km altitude to parlayse electronic system of the adversary. also, in august 2006, a Chinese ground-based laser has blinded a US reconnaissance satellite over China. As Ashley Tellis has aptly concluded, "...China's counterpace efforts are devise, comprehensive, rapidly improving, and deadly serious – exceeding even those of the Soviet Union as its peak. Taken together, Beijing space denial programs leave no doubt that it is determined to negate the operational advantages to Washington's space-enabled conventional military dominance.[68] He, therefore, argues that China will continue to invest in space-denial technology rather than subscribe to any arms control agreement that eliminates its chance of asymmetrically defeating superior American military power.

Sino-Pak Relations

China's nuclear proliferation to Pakistan is a crucial challenge before the international non-proliferation regime. China's nuclear cooperation with Pakistan involved all nuclear activities, conducting a nuclear explosion test for Pakistan, providing a nuclear weapon design, highly enriched uranium, setting up of a plutonium-production reactor at Khushab, reprocessing facility at Chashma, supply of crucial components like 5000 ring magnets (worth $ 70,000) and other critical components.

China's exports of M-11 short-range missiles (range 300 km and pay-load 500 kg) to Pakistan in 1990s created a major foreign policy challenge for the US on whether to impose sanctions on China or not. The US took a long time (till the year 2000) to conclude that China had transferred complete missile systems and technology to Pakistan. The 1990s were dominated by US sanctions on Chinese entities for violating the MTCR Category II guidelines. However, this was followed by waivers. In 1994, China signed a joint statement with the US that stated that it would not export ground-to-ground missiles in return for a waiver of sanctions by the US. On November 21, 2000 when the US government finally acknowledged that Chinese missile transfers did take place in the early 1990s to Pakistan and Iran, China issue another commitment not to export ballistic missile components and technology restricted by the MTCR in exchange for a US of sanctions for past missile transfers to Pakistan and Iran.

Despite its promise not to export missiles to Pakistan, Chinese support for the Pakistani nuclear program has continued unabated. In fact, China has followed a different route altogether. Instead of supplying missiles, China helped Pakistan achieve capability to develop missiles, which were termed by Pakistan as 'indigenous'. Pakistan started displaying a series of intermediate range ballistic missiles from April 1998 onwards when it test-fired the Ghauri missile (North Korean Nodong missile). This was followed by the short and intermediate range ballistic missiles viz., Shaheen I, Shaheen II, Ghaznavi, and cruise missiles viz., Abdali and Raad. As result of Chinese proliferation of nuclear, chemical and missile related technologies, the US sanctioned Chinese entities several times since 1970s.

China links most of its strategic concerns to the US policies and expects it to be sensitive towards China's concern. China on one hand makes statements about maintaining the sanctity of the non-proliferation regime while on the other hand gradually violates its obligations. Chinese nuclear and missile proliferation to Pakistan, Iran and North Korea cannot be done without government approval. China's proliferation to Iran is directed towards obtaining oil resources and oil exploration rights on a preferential basis while Iran relies on China for missile technology and support in easing sanctions. It gets oil from Saudi Arabia for exchange of missiles. China's protection to the North Korean military regime is also to further its strategic interests in the region. China's pursuit of its own interest over the larger global non-proliferation goals has significantly weakened the nuclear non-proliferation regime. China's selective adherence to the NPT in the future would not only erode its credibility as a responsible player but would also destabilise the regional order in Asia.[69]

Implications for India

China's economic and technological growth in the past three decades and its possible implications for the international system has long been debated in both academic and government circles. It is not known how China might behave in the coming years, whether it will be a responsible and cooperative player or it will use its military and economic might to safeguard its national interest thereby giving rise to challenges and threats to various countries. China's military and space modernization programmes will pose serious security challenges for various countries. It is possible these actions might force some countries like South Korea, Japan to review their nuclear and space policies. The 2007 ASAT test, ballistic missile test of 2010, successful flight-test of the space plane and anti-ship ballistic missile test in 2011 have caused doubts and suspicion on Chinese intentions.

The emergence of China as the second biggest economy in the World and its new status as a competitor to the US might force some Asian countries to revisit their security strategies, thus making way for new alliances.

The Sino-Pakistan nuclear and missile co-operation continues to pose threats to India. Chinese open policy of supporting Pakistan and its non-compliance with its obligation under the multilateral regimes like the NSG raise serious concerns about its future behavior for other countries in general and India in particular support to expose the Pak-China nexus and also to limit their cooperation.

China has managed to receive advanced technology transfers together with import of nuclear power reactors to its civil program. It is also eyeing the growing nuclear reactor market and plans to emerge as a major exporter of these technologies. India should not lag behind in this area.

Though China supports global nuclear disarmament, but there are no indications that China will unilaterally reduce the size of its nuclear arsenal. China calls on the US and Russia to reduce their arsenal to significant levels for it to join the nuclear arms reduction talks. On the issue of FMCT too, though China supports the treaty, it is believed to be supporting Pakistan in disrupting the proceedings at the CD.

Despite similarities in their policies regarding the 'no-first-use' policy and minimum nuclear deterrent and disarmament, yet differences persist between India and China on a number of issues. Chinese reluctance to accept India as a State with nuclear weapons despite the clean waiver from the NSG in which China is a party, is a concern in India. The US' call to integrate India into the global nuclear non-proliferation regime through the membership of NSG along with MTCR, Australia Group and Wassrnaar Arrangement is likely to face stiff opposition from China. There is need for a constructive dialogue between them to clear the differences.

There is a trust deficit between China and India on the approach to each other. China views India's engagement with the US as an Indian strategy to contain the growing stature of China, while many in India opine that China is determined to limit India to South Asian region through its association with Pakistan.

India needs to build requisite capabilities in order to strengthen its nuclear deterrent vis-à-vis China, even as it continues diplomatic engagements with Beijing, including at the nuclear level. The Indian and Chinese nuclear doctrines have several similarities and every attempt must be made to foster greater strategic stability through better understanding of each other's nuclear threat perceptions and capabilities.[70]

References

1. Fogg, Erik, "The Chinese Nuclear Weapons Program and its Threat to the United States and her Allies" December 6, 2006 (*http://web.mit.edu/efogg/Public/chinanuclear.pdf*).
2. Lewis, Wilson John and Litai, Xue, China Builds the Bomb (USA: Stanford University Press, 1988), pp. 2-10.
3. Nuclear Weapons Archive. "China's Nuclear Weapons." (*http://nuclearweaponarchive.org/China/ChinaArsenal.html*).
4. Fogg, Erik, n.1.
5. China has fomented insurgencies in the north-eastern states of India. But its direct involvement in these has declined over the years. It has instead found a more effective means of keeping India preoccupied by using Pakistan, its strategic ally, to keep the Indian Army embroiled with Pak-fomented sub-conventional conflict through a high level of cross-border terrorism.
6. Sethi, Manpreet, Nuclear Deterrence in Second Tier Nuclear Weapon States: A Case Study of India, Occasional Paper (New Delhi: Centre de Sciences Humaines, 2009), pp. 30-31.
7. John K. Fairbank, "Varieties of the Chinese Military Experience," in Frank Kierman and John K. Fairbank (eds.),

Chinese Ways in Warfare (Cambridge MA: Harvard University Press, 1974), p. 7

8. Thomas Cleary (trans.), The Art of War: Sun Tzu (Boston: Shambhala, 1988), p. 19.
9. Johnston, lain, Alastair China's Militarized Interstate Dispute Behaviour 1949-1992: A First Cut at the Data, The China Quarterly, March, 1998,p.7.
10. Ibid.
11. Chong-pin, Lin, "China's Nuclear Strategy: Tradition within Evolution"(USA: Lexington Books, 1988), p 19.
12. Johnston Iain Alastair, Cultural Realism: Strategic Culture and Grand Strategy in Chinese History (Princeton: Princeton University Press, 1995), pp. 63-65, 117-123.
13. Lau,D.C.,"Some Notes on Sun Tzu" Bulletin of the School of Oriental and African Studies, 1965 as cited by Rajain Arpit, "Nuclear Deterrence in South Asia-China, India and Pakistan", (New Delhi; Sage Publications, 2005), p, 107.
14. The Japanese war in the late 1930s is an exception.
15. Sun Tzu,"The Art of War", Trans. Lionel Giles, 1910,(*http://webcache.googleusercontent.com/search?q= cache:http://www.fas.org/man/artofwar.htm*).
16. Kondapalli, Srikanth, "China's Military: the PLA in Transitions", (New Delhi: Knowledge World 1999), p, 56.
17. G John Ikenberry, "Hegemony or Balance of Power? Regional Order and Conflict in a Transforming Asia", Asian Security Conference, IDSA, February, 2010.
18. Johnston, n.12.
19. Jing Dong Yuan, "China's Defense White Paper 2006", WMD Insights, February 2007, 1.(*http://www. wmdinsights.com/I12/I12_EA1_ChinasDefenseWhitePaper.htm*). Accessed 2 November 2010.
20. China's National Defense in 2006, "Section 2 – National

Defense Policy",(*http://www.china.org.cn/english/ features/book/ 194485.htm*).

21. Wang Zhongchun, "Nuclear Challenges and China's Choices", China Security, Issue No. 5 (Winter 2007), 61.

22. Cheng Guagjin, "Nuclear Strategy No Threat to Neighbors", China Daily, 23 April, 2010, URL: *http://www/chinadaily.com.cn/ cndy/2010-04/23/content_9764945.htm*

23. Shulong Shu and Yu Rong, "China: Dynamic ·Nuclear Detterent", in Muthiah Alagappa (eds.),, The Long Shadow: Nuclear Weapons and Security in 21st Century Asia, 2008 Stanford University Press, Stanford, California.

24. Litai Xue, "Evolution of China's Nuclear Strategy" as cited by John C., Strategic Views from the Second Tier in Hopkins and Weixing Hu ed, "The Nuclear Weapons Policies of France, Britain, and China" (University of California at San Diego, 1994) p. 171

25. Bruce Blair, "General Zhu and Chinese Nuclear Preemption", China Security, issue 1, Autumn 2006, p. 16.

26. As cited by Jeffrey Lewis, The Minimum Means of Reprisal: China's Search for Security in the Nuclear Age (Cambridge, Mass: MIT Press, 2007), p. 79.

27. Sethi, Manpreet, n.6. pp. 34-35.

28. Johnston Iain Alastair, "Prospects for Chinese Nuclear Force Modernization: Limited Deterrence Versus Multilateral Arms Control," China Quarterly, June 1996, pp. 552-58; and "China's New 'Old Thinking': The Concept of Limited Deterrence," International Security, vol. 20, no. 3, Winter 1995/96.

29. Bates Gill, James Mulvenon, Mark Stokes, "The Chinese Second Artillery Corps: Transition to Credible Deterrence", in Mulvenon, Andrew, N.D. Yang, eds. The People's Liberation Army as an Organization: Reference, volume V (2001), p. 548-49.

30. Evan Medeiros, "Evolving Nuclear Doctrine", in Paul J Bolt and Albert Willner, eds. China's Nuclear Future (London: Lynne Rienner, 2006) p. 41.

31. Chellaney,Brahma, The India-Pakistan-China Strategic Triangle and Role of Nuclear Weapons, Institut Français des Relations Internationals (IFRI) (France, Proliferation Papers 2002), p.22.

32. Neill, A, Donald, China's Evolving Nuclear Posture, (Canada: Defence R&D, Centre for Operational Research and Analysis, Sept 2011), p,56.

33. "China, Nuclear Weapons, and Arms Control: A Preliminary Assessment" (Washington, DC: Council on Foreign Affairs, 2000), pp. 34-35.

34. Neill, A, Donald, n.32. p.63.

35. "The Atomic Bomb: Statement of the Government of the People's Republic of China, October 16 1964".

36. China's National Defence White paper released in 2011.

37. Chellaney, Brahma, n.31.

38. Jonathan D. Pollack, "The Future of China's Nuclear Weapons Policy", in John C. Hopkins and Weixing Hu, eds., Strategic Views From the Second Tier: The Nuclear Weapons Policies of France, Britain, and China (New Brunswick:Transaction Publishers, 1995), p.159, quoted by the Nuclear Threat Initiative, (http://www.nti.org /db/china/nfuorg.htm).

39. Gupta, Arvind, China's Defence White Paper 2013: Lessons for India, IDSA Comments, April 25, 2013, (*http://idsa.in/idsacomments/ChinasDefenceWhitePaper2013Lessonsfor India_agupta_ 250413*).

40. Chellaney, Brahma, n.31.p.23.

41. Zhang Hui, n.2, p.142.

42. Annual Report to Congress: Military Power of People's Republic of China, US Dept of Defence, 2009 (*http://www.defence.gov/pubs/pdf/China_Military_Power_ Report_ 2009. pdf*).

43. Ibid.
44. Ibid, n. 42.
45. Joseph Cirincione, "China's Nuclear Modernization", Carnegie Proliferation Brief, Vol.2, No.8.(*http://www. carnegieen dowment.org/publications/index.cfm? fa=view&id=93*)
46. Missiles of the World, CSS-X-10, (*www.misiletheat.com/missile oftheworldid.35/missile_detail.asp*).
47. Guide to Military Equipment and Civil Aviation, (*www. deagel.com/ballistic-missiles/DF-41a000986001.aspx*).
48. Ibid, n.42.
49. M Kristensen, "New Chinese SSBN Deploys Hainan Island", April 24, 2008 (*http://www.fas.org/blog/ssp/2008/04/new-chinese-ssbn-deploys-to-hainan-island-naval-base.php*).
50. Huang Qiang, "Overseas Predictions about China's Latest Nuclear Submarine", Binggong Keji, September 2007, p.29
51. "Navy: China Bolsters Ballistic Missile Subs," Agence France-Press,(*http://www.defensenews.com /story/php?F=2594646&C= America*).
52. Cristopher McConnuaghy, "China's Undersea Nuclear Deterrent: Will the US Navy Be Ready?" in Lyle J. Goldstein, ed., China's Nuclear Force Modernisation, Newport, RI: Naval War College, 2006, p.43.
53. "China's Tests JL-2 SLBM", Washington Times, June 20, 2005,(*http://www.washingtontimes.com/ news/2005/jun/21/ 20050621-102521-5027r/*).
54. Andrew S. Erickson, Michael S. Chase, "China's SSBN Forces: Transitioning to the Next Generation Publication", China Brief, 9 (12), 2009, (*http://www.jamestown.org/single/?no_cache= 1&tx(tt_news) =35120&tx_ttnews[backpid)=7&cHash= b5b81 f14b8*).
55. "China Testing Ballistic Missile Defence System", The Donga-Ilbo, March 26, 2006.

56. "China reaffirms that its missile interception test defensive", Xinhua News Agency, January 12, 2010.

57. Jeffrey Lewis, "Chinese Missile Defense Test", Arms Control Wonk, January 12, 2010, (*http//lewisarmscontrolwonk.com/archive/2588/Chinese-missile-defense-test#comments*).

58. Ibid. p.3

59. Information Office of the State Council, of the People's republic of China, China's National Defense in 2004, December 2004, Bejing (*http://www.china.org.cn/e-white/20041227/index.htm) and China's National Defence in 2008, (http://www.china.org.cn/government/central_government/2009-01/20/content _17155577.html*).

60. Gray Mortimer, "Monkey see- Monkey Do-China & Russia building space plane too", UAS News, 30 January 2011.

61. As cited by Thomas M. Kane, "Dragon or Dinosaur: Nuclear Weapons in a Modernizing China," Parameters, winter 2003-04, p.101. Japan received a rating of four and India was at one.

62. Robert S. Norris and Hans Kristensen, "Chinese Nuclear Forces, 2008" Bulletin of Atomic Scientist, vol.64, July-August 2008, pp.42-44.

63. Ibid, pp.35-40

64. Centre for Non-proliferation Studies, Monterey, "China's Nuclear Weapon Development, Modernization and Testing," China Profiles, (*http://www.nti.org/db/china*).

65. Ibid.

66. "China Successfully Tests Multi-Warhaed Missiles," Yomiuri Shimbum, February 8, 2003.

67. According to a report prepared by Michael Pillsbury for the US bipartisan China Economic and Security Review Commission that is based on writings of 20 Chinese military strategists, there are three books and seven dozen articles

going back a decade that advocate development of ASAT to covertly shoot down satellites to send a deterrent message. As cited by Vago Muradian, "China's Mystery Satellites: US Gauges Beijing's ASAT Strategy," Defence News, May 2, 2007.

68. Ashley Tellis, "Punching the US Military's 'Soft Ribs': China's Antisatellite Weapons Test in Strategic Perspective," Carnegie policy Brief, no.51, June 2007.

69. Gupta, Anil and Kapur, K D, "Emerging Asian Nuclear Environment – Implications for India", (New Delhi: Indian Pugwash Society Publication, 2012), pp. 177-178.

70. Ibid, pp. 179-180.

Index